THE LAST ATTACK

6. SS-Panzerarmee and the Defense of

Hungary and Austria

Revised Edition

By

William Alan Webb

Last Brigade Books

Last Brigade Books

180 Big Bell Loop

Eads, TN 38028

More Non-Fiction from William Alan Webb

Killing Hitler's Reich, The Battle for Austria 1945

Fight to the Finish: Essays on the American Civil War

Have Keyboard, Will Type: Hard Lessons, Learned Hard

Abstract: Following defeat in the Ardennes Offensive, Adolf Hitler and the German leadership faced the question of how best to use what little offensive firepower remained to them, as represented by the *6. Panzerarmee*.[1] The redeployment that followed baffled the German High Command at the time, and historians ever since. Hitler's obsession with protecting the last source of natural oil available to the Reich compelled this decision, one made against the strong opposition of his military advisers. The resulting offensive, code-named *Unternehmen Frühlingserwachen, Unternehmen Frühlingserwachen*, was a catastrophe for Nazi Germany, but a boon for postwar Europe. Heavily outnumbered and lacking supplies, especially fuel, the *6. SS-Panzerarmee* nevertheless delayed the Red Army long enough for American and British forces to occupy much of western and southern Austria. There is, therefore, a strong likelihood the presence in Austria of *6. SS-Panzerarmee* saved that country from being overrun completely by the Red Army, and possibly being included in the Warsaw Pact.

Foreword

This essay and is meant to be a brief introduction to a largely unknown campaign at the end of the Second World War, which centered around the only Waffen-SS army level command ever

---

[1] For most of its existence, that army was officially known as *6. Panzerarmee*, without the 'SS' designation. Late in the war the Germans began referring to it as *6. SS-Panzerarmee*, and that is how it is most commonly known in western histories. To avoid confusion that is the designation that will be used here.

created. As such, it is primarily an overview of Hitler's reasons for ordering *6. SS-Panzerarmee* to participate in *Ünternehmen Frühlingserwachen*, the offensive to drive the Russians back behind the eastern bank of the Danube and thereby secure the Hungarian oil fields at Nagykanizsa. Small though they were those fields represented one of Germany's last sources of oil.[2]

Many otherwise well-read students of history are unfamiliar with this critical last phase of the Second World War on the Eastern Front. Those who study the war may already know much of what is included here, since the stated purpose of this essay is to serve as a primer for the fighting in Western Hungary and Eastern Austria in 1945. It is not a 'book' in the sense of having a comprehensive description of this period, and those who expect that it is will be disappointed.

And yet, many who have studied earlier works may have embedded ideas that no longer hold up in the face of new evidence. Either way, perhaps this will whet the appetite of those who are curious to learn more. By its very nature it is a summation only, a gateway for further study.

When writing such an essay, style becomes important. Veteran students of dense military histories expect a plethora of minute details that fit into a larger context. Casual readers unused to

---

[2] Contrary to what is often written, they were not the last oil fields in German hands, not even the most potentially productive. Those were in Austria.

following such a narrative can find that tedious. I have therefore attempted a middle style combining aspects of both. It's the style I shoot for in my fiction and is well liked in those books.

Another decision was what to include here. I chose to concentrate more on a strategic view than a tactical one, and to give a general overview of the topic. Sadly for historians, original sources for this period are few and far between. This essay has been revised using sources unearthed during my research for *Killing Hitler's Reich, The Battle for Austria 1945.*

This revision was called for because of new research in the field, not least by me; when you spend 13 years immersed in the events of a solitary month in 1945, if you dig deep enough you can uncover new material overlooked or ignored by your predecessors. At the time it was first written there was *no* definitive history of *6. SS-Panzerarmee* in the aftermath of the Ardennes Offensive. Georg Maier's flawed but highly detailed *Drama Between Budapest and Vienna, The Final Battles of 6. SS Panzer Armee* covered much of this ground, but the price for that edition was (and is) high. That book remains the gold standard for a history of the *6. SS-Panzerarmee* in 1945 and it also contains an excellent account of the fighting during the three *Konrad* attacks to relieve Budapest during January. But its price, generally more than $100 US, and enormous size, present an obstacle for many readers. It also effectively ends on March 31, 1945, the last day for which the *kriegstagebuch*, the War Diary for *Heeresgruppe Süd*, later *Heeresgruppe Ostmark*, is available. Nevertheless, Maier was the IA for *6. SS-Panzerarmee*. In the German command system, this placed him at the heart of the army, so that he was personally on hand to observe all reports and decisions. For example, all discussions of the infamous Cuff Band Order begin with Maier, who read the message at *6. SS-Panzerarmee* headquarters before anyone else.

He wrote his book in response to other postwar essays and memoirs written by German Army officers, largely for the US Army's World War II Foreign Military Studies Program. Those men tended to tell the Americans what they wanted to hear, and the participants had a natural tendency to shift blame to those who couldn't defend themselves. Almost as a matter of course they blamed the Waffen-SS for much that went wrong. In particular, he heaped scorn on *Generaloberst* Hermannn Balck, who commanded *6. Armee* on the left flank of *6. SS-Panzerarmee* in Hungary, and on its right flank in Austria. Balck's own self-serving memoir blamed the SS for the calamity, while praising his own skills for holding the front together. Balck *did* do a remarkable job of patching together his shattered army, but his over-the-top attack on *6. SS-Panzerarmee* so angered Maier that he wrote a rebuttal. When Maier sticks to the facts, his book comes across as a blow-by-blow account of the pivotal four months of February-May, 1945.

Some critics, with insufficient understanding of the sources available and not available to the researcher, display their misconceptions by reading a bibliography and judging the merit of a work based on what *they* think the author should have used. For most of Germany's experience during the Second World War we have extensive and detailed records, since the Wehrmacht[3] by and large kept meticulous records, but as the war drew to its inevitable end, previously rigid reporting standards fell by the wayside. Worse, most of the records that *were* written wound up being destroyed, either to deny them to the conquering Allies, or in the fighting. For example, the *SS-Führungshauptamt*, or the SS Main Office, which collated and archived all records from the Waffen-SS, was located in Berlin. When the capital fell, records were destroyed wholesale. Thus, for example, we know very little about the division-sized late war unit *SS-Kampfgruppe-Division Böhmen und Mähren*,[4] despite it having fought in combat from the moment it stepped foot on the battlefield. With more than 8,000 men on its rolls, divided into three regiments, the researcher cannot even be certain of what these regiments were named, or where exactly they fought. The author plans to write a brief history of this unit, but it will be largely based on anecdotal evidence because that's all we have.

For those who read German, a superb source on the fighting in Austria, and by extension *6. SS-Panzerarmee*, is Manfred Rauchensteiner's *Krieg in Österreich*. Rauchensteiner wrote his

---

[3] The word 'Wehrmacht' was the German equivalent of the American term 'Armed Forces.' It meant all branches, be they army, navy, air force, etc.
[4] This unit is sometimes erroneously identified as *31. Freilligen-Grenadier-Division der SS*. In fact, that division is the only SS division not to have an honorific title.

history of the fighting in Austria in the 1960s, when many surviving participants figured it was safe to discuss their experiences in the war, and those who had been imprisoned were released. The 1984 reprint has the same maps, which are beautifully done, although in the original 1970 edition they were individual fold-outs on a much larger scale.

For readers who wish for an in-depth exploration of the fighting in Hungary and Austria, the author suggests his own work, *Killing Hitler's Reich, The Battle for Austria 1945*. Topping 300,000 words and using more than 800 sources, written over 13 years and published in 2019 by Helion Books, the author believes that it will remain the definitive work on the Austrian campaign for the foreseeable future. This essay is an introduction, that book is comprehensive.

The saga of *6. SS-Panzerarmee* may come as a surprise to some, and it is the author's hope it inspires readers to seek more information on this complex subject. In particular there are some excellent new histories of *Unternehmen Frühlingserwachen*, although these tend to focus on the Waffen-SS panzer divisions and not the overall offensive. This is partly because of records destruction or the various units' inability to maintain proper records during the chaos of the times, and partly because no readily available unit histories exist of the Army panzer and infantry divisions that fought in Hungary. One of the most stories German formations of the war was *6. Panzer Division*, yet no decent unit history exists to chronicle its exploits. Earlier German editions are not available, yet *6. Panzer Division* remained heavily engaged with the Russians from January 1, 1945, through the end of the war.

For the new books, as might be expected some are excellent, some less so and some deeply flawed. Of necessity, this essay cannot distinguish between which is which for want of space, nor is that necessary for this work to be successful in its intent; the author has not used any but the best new works. If additional information is required by the reader, the bibliography included at the end of this manuscript is a good starting point for those wanting to know more. Here's hoping this motivates at least one person to do pursue further knowledge of this fascinating period. This is, after all, an introduction to this topic intended for those not already familiar with the subject.

Living in the digital age of publishing means errors in a manuscript can be corrected without delay. I know the vast community of Second World War historians, both professional and amateur, are quick to point out mistakes. Thus, this revised text is the result of a compendium of new research, discovered errors, reconsidered issues and revelations. Should the reader wish to discuss a particular part of this short work, please let the author know, either at his website, http://thelastbrigade.com/, or by email at webbwritingservices@gmail.com.

William Alan Webb, 16 February, 2021

A Note on Figures

Figures given in this work are based on what the author believes to be the best sources available. In the chaotic collapse of Nazi Germany, many records were lost or destroyed. For example, the *Kriegstagebuch* of *Heeresgruppe Süd* ends on March 31st, 1945. That is the formation to which *6. SS-Panzerarmee* was attached when the war ended.[5] Only fragments of daily reports are extant after that, with no hard numbers and only remnants of reports on the army's condition. We have good evidence that the records did exist at one time, but were lost or destroyed when the war end. Added to that are the often conflicting and incomplete figures quoted in the various histories, which are all more or less guesses; the later the period in the war, the less reliable are the figures. Once again, either the reports were lost, or units fighting for their lives and constantly on the move had no chance to compile them. Either way, reliable numbers are non-existent.

---

[5] As an interesting historical aside, the commander of *6. SS-Panzerarmee*, *SS-Oberstgruppenführer* Sepp Dietrich, briefly took over command of *Heeresgruppe Ostmark*, as *Heeresgruppe Süd* had been renamed, during the period May 7-8, 1945. *Generaloberst* Lothar Rendulic, the appointed commander, was captured by Americans on May 7, before the Army Group surrendered, and it fell to Dietrich to lead the group into captivity.

So what numbers *do* exist, and how close to authorized strength was the rebuilt *6. SS-Panzerarmee*? The answer is that we have good numbers up until about March 15, when the Russians launched their Vienna Offensive, and those numbers reflect a tank army at less than half strength in tracked vehicles.

First, it is appropriate to understand the authorized tank strength of a Waffen-SS panzer division in 1944. Sources can be found giving this number as everything from 120-140 tanks, to a high of 186. The reason for this is that even in the Waffen-SS, some formations tended to receive preferential treatment for replacements. Those bearing Hitler's name, *1 SS-Panzer Division Leibstandarte Adolf Hitler*, often referred to as the *LAH*, and *12. SS-Panzer Division Hitlerjugend*, therefore had Hitler's personal patronage. The oldest formation, *2. SS-Panzer Division Das Reich*, had the Nazi Party as a sponsor, and so on.

Taking this into account, even if the higher number of authorized *panzers*[6] is accepted as accurate, the reader is then faced with the case of *1. SS-Panzer Division Leibstandarte Adolf Hitler*, which had more than 200 Armored Fighting Vehicles (AFVs) on June 6, 1944, making it over-strength. And this does not even begin

---

[6] Although the classic *panzerkampfwagen* was a tank with a rotating turret, by 1944 the Germans used that term to indicate everything from a true panzer to an assault gun or *sturmgeschütz*, also including *jagdpanzers* or tank destroyers. The latter two types had fixed guns not mounted in turrets.

to address the case of the Army's *Panzer Lehr Division*, also with more than 200 AFVs.

Then in 1945, with new panzer production plummeting as factories were bombed out, overrun, or starved of essential materials, a series of reorganizations took place to distribute the remaining panzers among the existing divisions, further diluting their combat value.[7] The official table of organization for a 1945 Panzer Division, for instance, authorized a mere 45 panzers, which was less than a full battalion just a year earlier.

The numbers given in this work are therefore as accurate as the author feels is possible. In many cases they are from a German Army report, and may be accepted as being accurate. But others must be taken as educated estimates. Regardless, whether correct to the last panzer or not, they're close.

This is as true of manpower totals as it is of AFVs. Up until the very last day of the war, trainloads of men transferred from other services, or conscripted from theretofore exempt sources, showed up throughout the southern theater. Men bound for other destinations were pulled off trains and incorporated directly into burned-out divisions, all without proper records being kept. There is no way now to decipher the chaos into anything more than round numbers.

---

[7] The entire purpose of creating panzer divisions had been to concentrate an overwhelming amount of mobile firepower in one unit. Spreading them out among many units was how the French did it in 1940, and was a leading cause behind the Fall of France.

Following German defeat in the Ardennes Offensive, Adolf Hitler transferred *6. SS-Panzerarmee* to Hungary, ostensibly to protect Germany's last sources of natural oil. Whether that was the only reason, or even the *main* reason, remains unknown even today.

In doing so, Hitler altered the course of the war in Europe during the final months of fighting in 1945. To understand his motivation might be asking too much; Hitler's mind remains unknowable. And given Germany's dire economic straits and severely damaged transportation infrastructure at the time, not to mention the urgent need for fuel to keep its war machine running, the decision to deploy the army to Hungary made some sense at the time. Not enough to actually transfer the army, perhaps, but having a discussion about the best way to protect the Hungarian and Austrian oilfields had merit.

To understand the debate, it is first necessary to understand the context. By January of 1945, after Germany lost most of her remaining armored forces in the Battle of the Bulge, there could be no doubt to anyone on either side that Allied victory was only a matter of time. Six months earlier the twin disasters of summer, 1944, left Germany reeling, those being the successful Allied invasion of France, and the crushing defeat of *Heeresgruppe Mitte* by the Red Army in Operation Bagration. Those catastrophes left no question in the mind of anyone but the most fanatical Nazi that the

Third Reich had irretrievably lost the war. And aside from those deluded few who still believed that Hitler would manufacture a miracle, nobody doubted that defeat would come sooner rather than later; except, perhaps, Hitler himself. Like his mind, the truth of that is now unknowable.

Outwardly, however, Hitler took every measure he deemed possible to win the war, and to that end, one thing he did get right was that Germany could not win a defensive war. In that he was correct. The overwhelming materiel might of the Allies made any losses the Germans inflicted quickly replaceable, while Germany was fast running out of everything needed to wage war, but Hitler *did* profess that the war could still be won through attacks, and considered in its broadest sense that was true. In context, of course, it was false, because nothing Germany did could avoid final defeat. Given that Hitler refused to even consider that possibility however, and since a defensive war could not lead to victory that left attacking as the only alternative.

Leaving the initiative to the Allies meant they could strike at a place of their time and choosing. For example, Hitler's idea for the counterattack behind the Ardennes Offensive was sound. Punching a hole in the American front and turning north toward Antwerp might well have resulted in a replay of 1940…if the Wehrmacht had had the forces to accomplish the goal, but therein lay the rub. The German Army did not have such power, and hadn't had such power for years, if indeed it ever had. Even at the peak of its strength, the

Luftwaffe would have been hard-pressed to challenge the Allied air power of late 1944. Yet winning the war in December of 1944 by standing on the defensive would have required that the Germans to inflict a 3 or 4-1 loss ratio on the Allies, and that was impossible if the Allies held the initiative. So regardless of the imbalance of power, Hitler saw an offensive as the only choice.

Remarkably, the first days in the Ardennes crushed the American front line and resulted in the near-total destruction of the 106th Infantry Division. Withdrawing to safety at that point would have led to a significant tactical victory with minimal loss to the Germans, but of course, all such tactical victories only delayed the inevitable, as we can safely assume that Hitler knew. What Germany needed was the very thing she no longer had the power to achieve, a crushing strategic victory that would turn the tide of the war and give her a respite in which to recover.

It is significant that launching *5. Panzerarmee* and *6. SS-Panzerarmee* into the Ardennes never had much support in the German General Staff. They preferred to keep one army on the Western Front to counterattack Allied offensives, and to ship the other east to perform the same function against the coming Russian offensive in Poland, which the German's Eastern Front Intelligence Department, *Fremde Herren Ost*, Foreign Armies East, indicated would occur near the middle of January, 1945. Plans for a smaller version of the Ardennes Offensive were rejected by Hitler.

The generals had spent their careers learning how to win on the battlefield, and when that became no longer possible, they sought to use diminishing resources in the manner that best gave their armies a fighting chance not to be overwhelmed. Those were perhaps laudable goals, but Hitler had already decided that only through attacking could his regime survive.

Once those two armies suffered ruinous losses in the Ardennes Offensive, the debate then became what to do with the survivors. Conventional thinking was to rebuild the SS formations to whatever degree possible, and then send them north to defend Berlin. The Waffen-SS was, after all, *not* part of the German Army, but instead was the armed wing of the Nazi Party. Given that Hitler embodied everything the Third Reich stood for, defending his life made perfect sense as the *raison d'etre* for the Waffen-SS. After all, the SS had originated as Hitler's bodyguards, and the *Leibstandarte Adolf Hitler* supplied his personal guard battalion. Yet defending Berlin would only delay the end not prevent it, so Hitler chose yet another ill-advised offensive to change the course of the war. This time, he chose Hungary.

Contrary to what is now believed, the transfer did not come as a total shock to Hitler's military advisers. As early as December, 1944, before the Ardennes Offensive, Hitler favored a counterattack on the Red Army then moving into Western Hungary, using the land bridge between Lakes Balaton and Velence as the base. That was the now virtually unknown *Unternehmen Spätel*. The intention was to drive into the flank of the Russian spearheads driving west toward the oil fields at Nagykanisza, and then to turn east and regain the western bank of the Danube. And like most of Hitler's ideas, once he decided on one, he would press until it happened, and happen it did; twice.

Before those attacks however, the transfer of *6. SS-Panzerarmee* was adamantly opposed by the German officers charged with holding back the enemy forces then overrunning Germany. By late January, 1945, when the transfer began, they had already protested the transfer of *IV. SS-Panzerkorps* from Poland to Hungary for the Konrad operations, which were aimed at liberating the surrounded Budapest garrison. *IV. SS-Panzerkorps* was the chief mobile reserve for *Heeresgruppe Mitte*, in anticipation of a Russian Offensive through Western Poland toward Silesia and Berlin. *Fremde Heeren Ost*, the German Intelligence Agency, had developed an accurate picture of what forces the Red Army had available and when to expect the offensive, but Hitler dismissed the reports out as being the delusions of a madman.

Unfortunately for the Germans, they were remarkably accurate. Not that *IV SS-Panzerkorps* would have made much difference, since its two core divisions, *3. SS-Panzer Division Totenkopf* and *5. SS-Panzer Division Wiking* only had 20 percent of their armored strength, a combined total of less than 100 AFVs. Regardless, without *IV. SS-Panzerkorps*, the Red Army rolled over the weak German divisions defending Upper Silesia, who resisted fiercely but without enough firepower to stop the Russians.

Throwing *6. SS-Panzerarmee* into a counterattack wasn't a realistic option, since the army wasn't finished rebuilding until February. Indeed, all of its units hadn't fully disengaged from fighting the Americans until the Russian offensive in Poland had been raging for a week. Throwing the remnants of *6. SS-Panzerarmee* against the Red Army steamroller might have temporarily slowed the Russian offensive, but likely would have resulted in the final destruction of *6. SS-Panzerarmee*. Given its weakness even after being rebuilt, it was no long strong enough to do more than make the Russians pay a heavy price for their victory; before being rebuilt it was the equivalent of no more than a solitary panzer division.

But protests against launching *6. SS-Panzerarmee* back into combat without enough time to rebuild and train replacements fell on deaf ears, since the plan to send it to Hungary was the brainchild of the only man that mattered: Adolf Hitler. But that led to other problems. Transporting the most heavily armored army remaining in the German Order of Battle such a distance strained transportation resources to the breaking point. Compounding the difficulties, the need for secrecy required a tremendous deception effort. In the eyes of the German General Staff it was almost criminally superfluous to the protection of Germany…and yet, the fighting *6. SS-Panzerarmee* did in Hungary prevented the total conquest of Austria by the Red Army,[8] along with all of the ramifications that might have entailed.

And while *6. SS-Panzerarmee* was shattered in the process and suffered heavy casualties, it never collapsed. As mentioned previously, not only did the army commander, *SS-Oberstgruppenführer* Sepp Dietrich, became the commander of *Heeresgruppe Ostmark*, by the end of the war he also had the largest concentration of Waffen-SS divisions ever assembled in one area under his command.[9] Those included *1. SS-Panzer Division Leibstandarte Adolf Hitler*; a regiment from *2. SS-Panzer Division Das Reich*; *3. SS-Panzer Division Totenkopf*; *5. SS-Panzer Division Wiking*; *9. SS-Panzer Division Hohenstaufen*; and *12. SS-Panzer Division Hitlerjugend*, along with other SS-Divisions including *13. Waffen-Gebirgs-Division der SS Handschar*; *14. Waffen-Grenadier-Division der SS Galizien*; *16. SS-Panzergrenadier-Division Reichsführer- SS*; *17. SS-Panzergrenadier Division Götz von Berlichingen*; *18. SS-Freiwillige-Panzergrenadier-Division Horst Wessel*; *25. Waffen-Grenadier-Division der SS* Hunyadi; *26. Waffen-Grenadier-Division der SS Hungaria*;[10] *37. SS-Freiwillige-*

---

[8] That topic is too large for this essay. See the author's book *Killing Hitler's Reich, The Battle for Austria 1945* for a full discussion of the evidence for this theory.

[9] This occurred in the closing hours of the war, when advancing American units captured the Army Group Commander, Colonel General Dr. Lothar Rendulic, before active operations were due to cease. As the man on the spot, Dietrich took over as de facto commander.

[10] The Hungarian divisions were not combat ready and did not follow orders to engage the oncoming Americans, but are included here because they were stationed mostly in Austria at the time, and *Heeresgruppe Ostmark* was the only functioning headquarters in the area. Small parts of both divisions did skirmish with advance

Kavallerie-Division Lützow;[11] and the remnants of one regiment from *SS-Kampfgruppe Division Böhmen und Mähren*. Some of the units that fought until they were burned out skeletons had been freshly filled up with manpower in the last week of April and first week of May.[12] Despite the new men having little combat value due to lack of weapons and training, on paper there were more than 100,000 Waffen-SS men near the German border south of Linz.

The military realities of Germany's situation in mid-January, 1945, were grim. Even as it became obvious the great Ardennes Offensive had failed, Adolf Hitler refused to admit the plan had been a mistake. As fighting from *Unternehmen Wacht am Rhein*, Operation Watch on the Rhine, tapered off, the German High Command faced the most important decision for the direction of the war in 1945; what to do with the two armies that had seen most of the combat? As always, Hitler looked to the offensive for Germany's salvation. Unwilling to commit his last offensive assets to a passive defense, he searched for an opportunity to strike the advancing Red Army in the east.

American forces, and both sides suffered casualties, but these incidents were not sanctioned by the Hungarian commanders.
[11] Primarily the remnants of *SS-Kampfgruppe Keitel*.
[12] *Hohenstaufen*, as one example, was over-strength with nearly 20,000 men on its rolls.

As previously mentioned, the idea of where to place two shattered armies so that Germany might stave off defeat seems beyond reason to the modern reader.[13] Nor was this point lost on the German High Command. Whether they said so or not, most high-ranking Wehrmacht officers knew defeat was inevitable, a point which was not isolated to just his military advisors; the vast majority of Germans knew it too. But at no point did *Hitler* admit the war was lost, and Hitler was the only one who mattered.

Those in Western Germany weren't even still under German control, their regions having already been overrun by the Allies. Hitler, however, never stopped thinking how to win. No matter how bad it looked, outwardly he never gave up belief in victory.

5. Panzerarmee and *6. SS-Panzerarmee* spear-headed the Ardennes Offensive, an attack designed at splitting Allied forces in Belgium and re-capturing Antwerp, forcing a second Dunkirk evacuation as happened in 1940. The offensive was well beyond German capabilities in late 1944 and failed at achieving any of its strategic goals. Indeed, t'he ill-considered attack cost Germany most of her remaining reserves of both manpower and material. Those were casualties Germany could not make good. Yet despite their heavy losses, those two armies remained vital to the German defense

---

[13] The value of the armies was more than simply their numbers of men and machines. The men operating those machines were veterans, and willing to fight. In the late war German Army, that alone made them valuable.

of the Reich, especially *6. SS-Panzerarmee*, the sledgehammer of Germany's mobile forces, although by late January of 1945 it was a hollow shell of its former power.

The commander of *6. SS-Panzerarmee, SS-Oberstgruppenführer* Josef 'Sepp' Dietrich, had risen through the ranks of the Waffen SS from commander of Hitler's personal bodyguard troop, then of the *Leibstandarte Adolf Hitler* as both a regiment and then a division, to commander of *I. SS Panzerkorps* and finally *6. SS Panzerarmee.* Dietrich's army contemporaries considered him to have been a good divisional commander, who was promoted two command levels beyond his competence. Certainly he had never had a higher military education, having served in the First World War as a Sergeant. Dietrich's personal bravery was never in doubt, though, as he'd won the Iron Cross in both Second and First Classes. This record closely mirrored Hitler's own, as both men served in the Bavarian Army and both won the Iron Cross. For an enlisted man in the First World War that was quite a feat.

After the war Hitler and Dietrich became friends, something all too rare for the Führer. During the Night of the Long Knives in 1934,[14] Dietrich personally commanded the firing squad that executed SA officers accused of treason. Indeed, Dietrich and Hitler became so close, that even after joining the Waffen-SS, Dietrich

---

[14] June 30, 1934, was when purged all high leaders of the *Sturmabteilung*, the brown-shirted SA headed by another of Hitler's close personal friends, Ernest Röhm.

often ignored the orders of his nominal superior, Heinrich Himmler, knowing that his relationship with Hitler prevented Himmler from taking action against him.

6. SS-Panzerarmme was built around the core components of *I.* and *II. SS Panzerkorps*, containing four of the previously mentioned panzer divisions. The Order of Battle for *I. SS Panzerkorps* had the only two SS units allowed use of Hitler's name in their honorific titles, *1. SS-Panzer Division Leibstandarte Adolf Hitler* (*LAH*) and *12. SS-Panzer Division Hitlerjugend. II. SS-Panzerkorps* included *9. SS-Panzer Division Hohenstauffen* and *2. SS-Panzer Division Das Reich.* Other units would be attached and released during the army's brief history, such as *Schwere-Panzer-Abteilung 509* equipped with Tiger II panzers, and *356. Infanterie Division*, but those four panzer divisions were the army's permanent components.

When Hitler returned to Berlin on January 16, 1945, from the Western Front headquarters where he had directed the Ardennes Offensive, the debate within the German High Command began in earnest of how best to use *6. SS-Panzerarmee.* Several versions of these discussions exist, including one from then Chief of the General Staff *Generaloberst* Heinz Guderian and the War Diary kept by Chief of the Armed Forces High Command Operations Staff, General Alfred Jodl,[15] from which Former Deputy Chief of

Operations for the *Oberkommando der Wehrmacht*[16] Walter Warlimont drew his research when writing his account of this debate in *Inside Hitler's Headquarters 1943-1945*.

Warlimont knew both men well, and his account not only reconciles events surrounding this decision, but rings true about those often-heated arguments. Warlimont writes that on January 16th, "Hitler ordered that *6. SS-Panzerarmee*...should be thrown into Hungary to protect the vital oil area."[17] Guderian launched vehement protests. "On hearing this I lost my self-control and expressed my disgust to Jodl in very plain terms..."[18] Guderian wanted *6. SS Panzerarmee* transferred north to defend Berlin. The argument lasted much of the day and in Guderian's words the "disagreements were violent."[19] Warlimont backs up Guderian's assertion with the words of *Generalfeldmarschall* Wilhelm Keitel[20], Chief of the Armed

---

[15] Chief of the Armed Forces High Command Operations Staff meant that Jodl took part in planning, authorizing and directing all German military operations.

[16] High Command of the Armed Forces.

[17] Warlimont, General W., *Inside Hitler's Headquarters 1939-1945*, (Novato: Presidio Press, 1990), pp. 499

[18] Guderian, H., *Panzer Leader,* (New York: Ballantine, 1968), pp. 321

[19] Guderian, Heinz, *Panzer Leader, The Classic Account of German Tanks in World War II – by the Commander of Hitler's Panzer Corps in Russia,* (New York: Ballantine, 1968), pp. 322

[20] As chief of the Armed Forces High Command, Field Marshal Wilhelm Keitel was, in theory, Hitler's highest ranking military advisor. His main qualification for this position was his disinclination to disagree with Hitler about anything. Behind his back he was nicknamed 'lakeitel', which in German means 'lackey.' In an ironic twist, his son was a member of the Waffen-SS and commanded a battle-group fighting in Hungary and Austria during the period in question, his unit (*Kampfgruppe Keitel*) being attached to *6. SS-Panzerarmee* on several occasions.

Forces High Command, whom Warlimont quotes as having said: "that Hitler *considered the protection of Vienna and Austria as of vital importance* and that he [Hitler] would *rather see Berlin fall than lose the Hungarian oil area and Austria.*"[21] (Author's italics)

In essence then, Guderian, while representing the top planning authority in the Army, wanted Dietrich's battered and only partially rebuilt command used to stop the Russian threat to Berlin. Weakened though it may have been after the Ardennes Offensive, it was still the strongest army left in the German Order of Battle, and according to Michael Reynolds, Sepp Dietrich agreed with Guderian..[22] Whether in a counter-attack from Pomerania[23], or as an armored reserve for Army Group Vistula[24], the two generals agreed that *6. SS-Panzerarmee* should move north. They argued their case with passion but to no avail since, according to Reynolds, "Hitler would have none of it."[25]

Referring to the previously mentioned discussion, Hitler believed Germany could not win the war by remaining on the

---

[21] Warlimont, *Inside*, pp. 499

[22] Reynolds, *Sons*, pp 247

[23] Such an attack took place anyway, without either I or I/ SS-*Panzerkorps*. Known as *Unternehmen Sonnenwende*, it had little firepower but managed to scare the Russian Supreme Command into clearing Pomerania before advancing on Berlin.

[24] The Soviet winter offensive came to a halt on the Oder River in January of 1945, leaving them some 60 miles from Berlin. Defending the western bank of the Oder, between the Red Army and the capital, was Army Group Vistula.

[25] Reynolds, Major General Michael, *Sons of the Reich, II SS Panzer Corps*, (Havertown: Casemate, 2002), pp 247

defensive; she simply was not strong enough to hold out much longer. Winning the war, therefore, meant attacking, trying to inflict so much damage on one or the other of her enemies they would give up the fight. Despite Guderian's protests, in Nazi Germany nothing mattered except Hitler's orders, and so, *6. SS-Panzerarmee* entrained for Hungary and prepared for offensive action.

Regardless of where *6. SS-Panzerarmee* moved, however, if it was going to be effective it first had to be re-built. According to Maier the SS panzer divisions sustained severe losses during the Ardennes Offensive, leaving them incapable of further offensive action.[26] Rebuilding the ruined units first required new manpower, and by this point in the war the voluntary nature of the Waffen-SS was long since forgotten. In desperation, young boys were drafted to fill the ranks. As the American handbook on the German military stated at the time concerning conscription of 16 year-olds "in the past 2 years a large proportion of the youngest age class has been induced by various kinds of pressure to volunteer, largely for the Waffen-SS."[27] Induced, in the parlance of Nazi Germany, meant conscripted, but drafting 16 year-olds could not, by itself, make good the losses. Germany had already scraped the bottom of the

[26] Maier, Georg, *Drama Between Budapest and Vienna, The Final Battles of 6th SS Panzer Army, 1945*, (Winnipeg: JJ Fedorowicz, 2004), pp 115-116

[27] *War Department Technical Manual TM-E30-451 Handbook on German Military Forces, 15 March, 1945,* pp I -57

manpower barrel to bring *6. SS-Panzerarmee* back up to strength after it was destroyed in Normandy. Because most of those replacements fell in Belgium, it became necessary to do it again but with even fewer resources.

The Second World War was very much a war of attrition. Manufacturing the material for prosecuting the war depended on workers standing long hours on the production lines. Every nation faced the dilemma of having finite numbers of people to fill the dual needs of both industry and the military. There is a myth that the Soviet Union had, for all practical purposes, an inexhaustible supply of manpower, but that was never true. The Red Army coerced Estonians, Latvians, Lithuanians, Rumanians, Bulgarians, Slovenes and Poles into their ranks, to compensate for the enormous losses suffered in the first three years of war. By the end, formations in the less critical portions of the Eastern Front were often reduced to skeletons.

In the free countries, utilization of manpower involved critical decisions about how large of a military force they could field. The United States, for example, made a conscious decision to limit the size of the army so the excess personnel could produce more weapons. Those weapons would then be employed en masse to overwhelm the enemy in a storm of steel, which has come to be known as The American Way of War. Women entered the work force for the first time and filled the critical void, freeing up men for military service. The social effects of this strategic decision would make great fodder for the right novelist.

Germany could not pursue this policy. Recent studies have illustrated her dire manpower status as early as 1941, before the invasion of Russia. The loss of 750,000 men in the first six months of the Russo-German War left Germany bereft of adequate replacements. Three years before the events of this book Germany was out of available men, and many of the commanders and divisions from 1942 onwards were not considered front line material. During the Battle for Velikiye Luki in 1942 for example, the commanding general of *331. Infantry Division* was so feeble he could not leave his headquarters, while the men under his command were overage reservists conscripted to fight partisans. Instead, they were pressed into service alongside first class formations.

Cannibalizing industry to make up the deficit would leave the Wehrmacht without the weapons those same men needed to keep fighting, although in the end this is what Germany resorted to doing, and on a grand scale. Unlike the United States, Germany was not bound by the restraints of morality. Slave labor from the conquered countries arrived en masse in the Reich to staff the factories, thus freeing up Germans for military duty.

The authorized ration strength of an SS panzer division in 1945 was approximately 19,000 men. That is, the total number of men including all sub-units such as supply, repair and combat. As might be expected, the combat units wore down quickly once engaged in fighting. To bring the divisions back up to strength, the Waffen-SS found replacements anywhere they could. Some of these were veteran SS men returning from leave or recovered from wounds, but many were surplus Luftwaffe and *Kriegsmarine*[28] men with no infantry training. A large percentage did not know how to clean the basic German infantry rifle, the K-98 Mauser. Until they could be trained by the division to which they were assigned, such men were useless in battle.[29]. Moreover, *6. SS-Panzerarmee* as a whole had a critical shortage of both officers and NCOs, meaning younger, less experienced men were promoted to fill positions for which they were not qualified. Finally, the once stringent Waffen SS acceptance standards had long since been forgotten, including the minimum height requirement. The asphalt soldiers of the early years were mostly gone by 1945.[30]

---

[28] The German Air Force and Navy.

[29] As the postwar American historian S.L.A. Marshall alleged in *Men Against Fire*, training men to shoot to kill another man, even an enemy, was more of an art than a science. Training could, however, offset experience when it came to things like maintaining unit coherence in the face of enemy action. Without even the basics of such training, the value of men unfamiliar with even how to use their personal weapon was minimal.

[30] Guillemot, Phillippe, translated from the French by Lawrence Brown, *Hungary 1944-45, The Panzers' Last Stand*, (Paris: Histoire & Collections, 2010), pp 69

But exactly how strong should an SS Panzer Division of this period have been? How strong were they? Revisiting a previous topic seems in order here to keep in mind the relative weakness of *6. SS-Panzerarmee* during the period under study.

The panzer forces had undergone numerous re-organizations since 1943, in an effort to maximize the effectiveness of a force that was increasingly out-numbered, making it difficult to establish precisely what their authorized strength was in early 1945. Compounding this, in the case of the Waffen-SS divisions was that some had patrons who could influence their priority for weapons and manpower[31]. Most sources agree, however, that on paper the total number of tanks, tank destroyers and assault guns, collectively referred to as armored fighting vehicles (AFVs), should have been somewhere near two hundred for the Waffen SS divisions, but far less for an ordinary Army panzer division.[32] Earlier in the war a distinction was made between panzers (tanks), with a rotating turret,

---

[31] As discussed above *Liebstandarte Adolf Hitler* and *Hitlerjugend* had Hitler himself as a patron. Thus they often had priority of scarce resources. *Das Reich* was also favored by Hitler because one of its *panzergrenadier* regiments had the honorific title *Der Führer*, and because it was the very first Waffen-SS unit.
[32] The final reorganization of the panzer forces in March, 1945, for example, limited such a division to a mere 40 tanks, roughly one quarter of what the authorized strength had once been. The SS divisions, however, did not fall under this reorganization plan, and few, if any, Army divisions were actually so changed. To confuse matters even more, by 1945 there was no practical difference in the authorized strength of a panzer division and a *panzergrenadier* division.

and vehicles with a fixed main battery such as a tank destroyer or assault gun, but the days for such specificity expired as the divisions grew progressively weaker. In June of 1944, for example, prior to the Normandy Invasion, *1. SS-Panzer Division Leibstandarte Adolf Hitler* boasted an AFV complement totaling 219 vehicles, while *12. SS-Panzer Division Hitlerjugend* had only 153, a difference of 66 AFVs for divisions with exactly the same Table of Organization and Equipment. Even with that disparity, this gave *I. SS-Panzerkorps* the impressive total of 372 panzers, tank destroyers and assault guns, more than all of *6. SS-Panzerarmee* would have nine months later when *Unternehmen Frühlingserwachen* was launched.

Continuing to use *1. SS-Panzer Division LAH* strength returns as an example for all of the Waffen-SS Panzer Divisions, according to Reynolds the returns for January 15, 1945 show a battered division that was a shadow of its former self. A mere 49 AFVs were ready for action after the Ardennes Offensive, made up of 29 Panthers[33], 18 Mark IVs and 2 *Jagdpanzer* IVs, but those Mark IVs all mounted the older 75/L48 main gun.[34] That gun had much

---

[33] The Panzer Mark V 'Panther' is considered by some the best overall tank of World War II. A medium tank with a high velocity 75mm main gun, the Panther incorporated much of the design of the Soviet T-34. It was feared by its enemies and deadly in the hands of a veteran crew, but also had ongoing mechanical problems that were never wholly solved.

[34] Reynolds, Major General Michael, *Men of Steel: I SS Panzer Corps, The Ardennes and Eastern Front, 1944-45*, (New York: Sarpedon, 1999), pp 157

less penetrating power than its successor, which was being installed on newer models.

The Panthers and *Jagdpanzer IV* tank destroyers were modern, effective vehicles with a main battery suited for combat against enemy armor. The Mark IV, on the other hand, was obsolescent by that point, having served in front-line duty since 1939. It could still be dangerous in the hands of a veteran crew, but its 75/L48 gun was only marginally effective against the new Soviet heavy tanks of the JS-I and JS-II types. It fared little better against the newest incarnation of the famous T-34, the T-34/85. Only against the American Sherman did it still favorably compare.

And while reinforcements would shortly join *LAH*, even a cursory comparison to the number of AFVs from seven months before shows just how badly the division had fared during the fighting in France and Belgium. Worse, some of the vehicles still on hand after the Ardennes Offensive had been repaired more than once, and were balky and unreliable. By March 1, after being rebuilt and participating in *Unternehmen Südwind*,[35] the *LAH* combat-ready AFV strength had again fallen to a mere 74, barely a third of what it had been 9 months earlier, and only 25 vehicles more than after the Ardennes Offensive debacle..

---

[35] Operation Southwind, the last successful Army sized German attack of the Second World War destroyed a Russian bridgehead on the west bank of the Gran River.

II. SS-Panzerkorps was in similar condition. Reynolds asserts that when the time came for *Unternehmen Frühlingserwachen* the Corps could field only "…185 tanks, *Jagdpanzers* and *StuGs* (assault guns), between them…50% below their authorized holdings."[36] Guillemot is more specific, giving the total number of AFVs for *2. SS-Panzer Division Das Reich* as 76 and for *9. SS-Panzer Division Hohenstauffen* as 77, for a total of 153.[37] Among the vehicles ready to fight, though, a great number were vehicles repaired by the Corps maintenance personnel and not newly manufactured. Put another way, a substantial number were war weary machines kept in service to maintain the numbers.

In SPWs[38], *Hohenstaufen* was well below strength with 167, while *Das Reich* had 258; *Das Reichs*[39] artillery component was close to full strength but *Hohenstaufen* was at half strength. In short, then, while *II SS-Panzerkorps* had close to its full complement of men, and in late winter of 1945 that in itself was unusual among

---

[36] Reynolds, *Sons*, pp 250
[37] Guillemot, *Hungary*, pp 73
[38] SPW is the abbreviation for *Schützenpanzerwagen*, literally 'protected armored vehicle'. The ubiquitous SPW was the German version of the American half-track. Designed to carry *panzergrenadiers* into battle and to offer a modicum of protection from small arms fire, the SPW came with a vast array of armaments, from a simple MG-34 or MG-42 machine gun, several different anti-aircraft versions, mortars and even one version that mounted a 75mm assault gun. SPWs were mainly assigned to the *panzergrenadier* regiment. Motorized infantry differed in that they were driven to the battle site in trucks.
[39] German grammar does not use a possessive apostrophe.

German units, in terms of actual combat power the Corps was nowhere near full striking power. Severe supply shortages plagued all German units.

The reconstruction of both *I.* and *II. SS-Panzerkorps* was supposed to have been finished by January 30, but in fact new equipment and recruits were still joining their divisions on the eve of *Unternehmen Frühlingserwachen* on March 6, 1945. Allied attacks on Germany's rail system slowed all movement to a comparative crawl.[40] Strategic bombing of German industry made construction of new weapons problematic, not to mention crippling synthetic oil production. This meant logistic support for *6. SS-Panzerarmee* was sporadic even with its high priority. Nor do numbers alone tell the entire story. Reynolds gives the manpower strength of *I. SS-Panzerkorps* just before *Frühlingserwachen* as the following: "...Das Reich was some 1000 men over and the Hohenstaufen only 1,200 men under the authorized strength of a Waffen-SS Panzer Division-approximately 18,500 of all ranks."[41] On paper, then, the divisions appeared more or less at full strength in manpower, a rarity for a German division in 1945. But as previously discussed, those numbers are very misleading, since so many of the replacements

[40] For those interested in data concerning German military transport capacity in the early and late war periods, and the requirements for transporting various types of units, see the author's *Killing Hitler's Reich, The Battle for Austria 1945.*
[41] Reynolds, *Sons*, pp 249-250

were untrained or undertrained in ground warfare, and many were well past military age.

What had not diminished was the morale of the SS formations. Reynolds marvels that, even in the last stages of the war, their attitude not only remained steadfast, but that it rubbed off on the new recruits from other branches of the Wehrmacht. "By February 1945 the soldiers of *I. SS-Panzerkorps* knew their country had no chance of winning World War II, but they were determined not to surrender 'unconditionally...'"[42] Morale in this case is defined as a willingness to follow orders from trusted officers, when the outcome of the war had already been decided.

Americans may wonder at this, since by this point discretion was most assuredly the better part of valor for most of the German Army. What motivated the SS men to keep fighting? Loyalty to the Führer had long since evaporated for most of them, so why not lay down their arms and surrender? Aside from betraying their comrades, something veterans could not imagine doing,, in their minds they fought to save their homes and families from being overrun by the Red Army. Germans held no illusions about what happened when the Red Army overran a town or city. Mass rape and murder filled their newsreels, and the old hands knew the Russians were out for revenge, so they fought to give more time for citizens to escape to the lines of the Americans and British.

---

[42] Reynolds, *Sons*, pp 251

Once the decision was firm to send *6. SS-Panzerarmee* to Hungary, elaborate deception measures were undertaken to hide it from Allied and Soviet intelligence so that its ultimate destination was unknown. The actions taken included removing cuff bands, giving combat formations innocuous code names[43] and some units were even routed through Berlin first before shipping them to Hungary. Given the dire condition of the German railway system, such ruses only added to the strain on men and machines, as the Waffen-SS men could see for themselves what the Allied Strategic Bombing Campaign had done to German. While on those detours, only the most senior officers knew their final destination. And for the most part the strenuous efforts made to keep the army's deployment a secret worked; the Soviets had no clear idea of where, or even if, *6. SS-Panzerarmee* was headed their way. As it turns out the Germans themselves betrayed their presence to the Russians.

Of course, none of the smoke and mirrors used to cover up the army's true destination mattered unless it arrived in Hungary in a timely fashion, and even when rolling stock and locomotives were available, the journey remained extremely dangerous. American and

---

[43] For example, *II SS-Panzerkorps* was called *SS-Ausbildungs Korps Süd*, SS Training Corps South. Cuff bands were removed to camouflage the units to which the men belonged. The irony of this was that they were never sewn back on, so that later, when Hitler ordered Cuff Bands removed as punishment for alleged poor performance, they were already gone.

British fighter-bombers roamed the western skies with impunity, shooting anything on wheels, with trains as especially high-value targets. The continuing damage to Germany's rail network was extreme. As an example of how this affected *6. SS-Panzerarmee*, Maier stated the move was accomplished at Tempo Four, that is, four trains every twenty-four hours. In 1940, similar moves were accomplished at Tempo Seventy-Eight, or twenty times faster.[44] German military trains had a uniform composition, and under ideal circumstances it took 110 trains to move a panzer division. It is not hard to extrapolate from those numbers that the German rail network operated at less than five percent of prewar efficiency in February of 1945.

Unfortunately for the Germans, the advantages accrued from the deception measures surrounding *6. SS-Panzerarmee*'s transfer to the Hungarian theater, were lost with the launching of *Unternehmen Südwind* on February 13. From the German viewpoint, the *Südwind* offensive was a mandatory prelude to Spring Awakening, and tactically it made sense. Strategically, however, it laid bare Germany's future offensive plans, giving the Russians a clear idea for how Hitler planned to defend the heartland.

The *Südwind* plan called for the German *8.Armee* to attack a large Soviet bridgehead north of the Danube and west of the Gran River, a dangerous position which the Red Army could have used as the assembly area for its own offensive aimed at Vienna, along the

---

[44] Maier, *Drama*, pp 116.

north bank of the Danube. Even more dangerous was the chance that Soviet units in the Gran bridgehead might have crossed the Danube from north to south, and from there drive into the rear of the German assault units involved in *Unternehmen Frühlingserwachen*. In order to ensure the attack's success, *8. Armee* asked for and was given the use of *I. SS-Panzerkorps*.

Südwind started in mid-February and the two Waffen SS divisions of *I. SS-Panzerkorps* made the critical difference in success or failure. The fighting was hard but the Germans finally cleared the entire Russian bridgehead on the west bank of the Gran. Soviet losses were substantial and the offensive was a clear-cut victory, the last one of the war for Germany. Guillemot gives Soviet losses as "2,069 men killed, 537 prisoners, 71 tanks and 134 guns destroyed as well as 24 others captured."[45] But while the use of the two 'Hitler' SS Panzer Divisions ensured victory in the preparatory offensive, it also betrayed their presence to the Soviets and made clear that the main German offensive effort would come in Hungary.

The moment *Südwind* kicked off, Soviet intelligence identified *I. SS-Panzerkorps* and correctly divined German intentions to launch a major offensive in Hungary. This came as both a surprise and a relief. They had totally lost track of where *6. SS-Panzerarmee* had been redeployed, and although it had ensured victory in *Südwind*, committing the SS divisions wasted the secrecy measures the Germans had gone to such extremes to put in place. Reynolds

---

[45] Guillemot, *Hungary*, pp 64

puts it this way: "...the use of *I. SS-Panzerkorps* in Operation Southwind was a serious mistake."[46] No longer was the location of *6. SS-Panzerarmee* unknown and its purpose in Hungary could not be mistaken. Panzer divisions had not been built for defensive purposes; the SS was there to launch an attack. Nor was the question of where in doubt, either, since the only strategic purpose could be to protect the oil fields. Correctly guessing the target area for *Unternehmen Frühlingserwachen*, the Soviets began doing what they did best, building defensive works.

Water and waterways defined the Hungarian battlefield. Two rivers swollen by winter rains outlined the zone of combat. First, running north-south out of Slovakia into Hungary was the Gran River,[47] which emptied into the Danube at the port city of Gran, called Esztergom in Hungarian. At this point the Danube bends from the roughly east-west course that takes it past Vienna and Bratislava, to the north-south course bisecting Budapest just southeast of Gran. On the southern side of the Danube after it has turned west toward Vienna are two lakes, Lake Velence and the much larger Lake Balaton, roughly west-southwest from Budapest. The land between those two lakes would be the springboard for *Unternehmen*

---

[46] Reynolds, *Sons*, pp 257

[47] Gran is the German name, while the Slovakian name is the Hron River. Gran is used here because that is the most common name used in German sources, which make up the majority of those available.

Frühlingserwachen, exactly as it had been six weeks earlier for *Unternehmne Konrad III*.

A few miles north-west of Lake Velence was the city of Stuhlweissenberg, Székesfehérvár in Hungarian. This small city had been a vital crossroads for centuries and would prove to be so again. When the Russians launched their Vienna Offensive, the German stand at Stuhlweissenberg would hold them up just long enough to prevent a total catastrophe, instead of merely a disaster.

Unternehmen Frühlingserwachen was the most poorly conceived German offensive of the Second World War. Given how inept others were that is a strong statement, but this author believes the facts back it up. *Frühlingserwachen* was unoriginal and, without question, unrealistic in the same way as the Ardennes Offensive. In essence it was a modified version of the failed *Konrad III* attack in January. In the early going *Konrad III* broke through to the Danube and came close to relieving the garrison of Budapest, but in the end the German forces proved too weak to sustain their gains. After burning out the assault units through losses, the Germans wound up retreating back to their starting lines. Just like the Ardennes Offensive, they spent irreplaceable German blood and war material for no advantage. The losses they inflicted, while severe, were poor compensation for the cost.

Worse, the momentary success of *Konrad III* inspired Hitler to double down on the plan by increasing the attacking forces. He ignored that Russian forces no longer tied down besieging Budapest and had reinforced the front and moved into defensive positions. He ignored the evidence of strong Russian field fortifications that would mow down the attackers and smash their AFVs. He ignored the pleas of his advisors not to waste Germany's very last offensive firepower on such a far-fetched and impossible plan. As always, Hitler ignored everything except his own intuition.

The basic plan for *Frühlingserwachen* called for *6. SS-Panzerarmee*, reinforced by *I. Kavallerie Korps*, and in conjunction with *III. Panzerkorps* from *6. Armee*, to drive south, southeast and east from the line between Lakes Balaton and Velence. This fan-shaped attack was intended to clear much of the west bank of the Danube below Budapest, as well as driving to meet forces from *Heeresgruppe E* driving north from the Drava River. The weak *2. Panzerarmee* would attack due east into the center of the Russian bulge, and the three attacking formations would then meet near Szekszárd and drive Third Ukrainian Front back across the Danube. That would clear the Red Army from a huge mass of Hungary and keep the oil fields near Nagikaniza safely in German hands. Like all of Hitler's ideas, on paper the plan looked workable, but the problems were legion and the chance of success nil.

For one thing, the forces available were wholly inadequate to the task at hand, particularly the infantry forces. Both *2.*

41

Panzerarmee and *Heeresgruppe E* had no AFVs to speak of,[48] so those attacks would not only make no headway, they would do little to draw Red Army reserves from the northern battlefield; the Russian defenses facing them proved adequate to stop their attacks cold. They added nothing to the offensive and merely wasted precious manpower.

As for the *schwehrpunkt*[49] there were no substantial follow-on units moving behind the assault elements of *6. SS-Panzerarmee* to secure the ground that was gained. This meant the attack units on either side of the offensive had to protect their own flanks. The further they moved into Soviet-held territory, the more strength they would have to peel off to guard against Russian counterattacks in their sides and rear. This self-limiting handicap meant the tip of the assault would grow progressively weaker as the assault made progress, even without accounting for casualties. Worse, as *6. SS-Panzerarmee* Commander *SS-Oberstgruppenführer* Sepp Dietrich knew, the further the attack moved south and east, the more vulnerable it became to an attack by the Soviet forces then massing south of the Danube near Gran.[50] They were, in effect, fighting their way into an ever-more-dangerous trap.

---

[48] *16. SS-Panzergrenadier Division Reichsführer SS*, did have a full battalion of *sturmgeschütz*, but of the three German AFV types they were the least effective against Russian armor.
[49] The main point of attack, literally 'heavy point.'
[50] Reynolds, *Sons*, pp 257

Strong Soviet forces north of Stuhlweissenberg faced *6. Armee*, commanded by *Generaloberst* Hermannn Balck, and 3rd Hungarian Army on Balck's left flank. Neither of those formations was strong enough to hold back the major Soviet offensive which German intelligence predicted for mid-March, and there were no reserves to seal off a breakthrough into *6. SS-Panzerarmee*'s rear. Even a cursory glance at a tactical map showed the folly of the *Frühlingserwachen* plan.

The weather in Western Hungary worked against any movement at all, much less an attack: heavy rains and temperatures just above freezing created deep mud throughout the battlefield region, which made even digging trenches problematic. One consequence was that not all units were in position to attack at the same time. *II. SS Panzerkorps*, for example, didn't not engage the Russians for nearly a day after the rest of *6. SS-Panzerarmee*. When March 6, the date of attack finally dawned, movement of vehicles anywhere except on the roads was impossible.

Off of few paved highways, the roads were strips of elevated dirt that became less passable as traffic increased, churning their surface into a sticky brown goo. Men walking cross-country found the going slow and clumsy, as deep mud sucked at their feet. John Toland tells of a certain panzer commander, one Fritz Hagen, who protested the ground was so saturated with water he could not attack, since he commanded tanks, not submarines." [51]

[51] This 'Fritz Hagen' is yet another SS nom de guerre, no doubt used to protect the identity of the man who even 20-plus years after the

As stated earlier, and cannot be overstated, nothing was surprising about such conditions, other than perhaps the timing. Heavy rains that turned whole regions of in Central Europe and European Russia into quagmires were semi-annual events. The Germans were faced with a normal weather pattern, "the onset of what is called 'razputitza', a three to four week period of almost complete immobility in Spring and Autumn due to muddy conditions..." [52] The same phenomenon stopped the drive on Moscow in 1941. Since the glue-like mud would either slow the German armored vehicles to a crawl or swallow them, the Soviets would have time to rush reinforcements and build defenses in whatever sector was under attack. In turn, the Germans would be forced to fight for every yard, making any foundering vehicles easy targets for dug-in Soviet anti-tank guns. Not only was blasting through deep fixed defenses a misuse of Germany's last offensive assets, but only a rapid breakthrough and exploitation gave the offensive any hope for success. The weather obviated this possibility.

After protesting vehemently against any attack, and being ordered to plan an offensive anyway, Hitler was presented with three

war ended feared prosecution. Verification of the story is, therefore, problematic. It is used here because the author feels its essential truth about the conditions makes a higher point, whether the story itself is apocryphal or not.
[52] Reynolds, *Sons*, pp 259

plans for *Unternehmen Frühlingserwachen* for his approval before the final version was decided upon. *6. SS-Panzerarmee* submitted one, drawn up largely by *SS-Obersturmbannführer* Maier as the Operations Officer, or IA, that called for a drive due south on a short and focused route that kept the assault units concentrated. The objectives of Maier's plan were achievable because they were small. They also would have protected the oil fields, at least in the short term, but would not have been the strategic victory that would change the course of the war. Under Maier's plan, though, *6 SS-Panzerarmee* would then have been available to redeploy in defense of Berlin. Hitler rejected it.

An alternative proposal by Hermann Balck was similar, and received the same reply. Neither would save the oil fields outright, because that was beyond Germany's remaining capabilities, but the idea was to delay their loss and that might have been possible. The plan Hitler wanted, however, was the one submitted by *Heeresgruppe Süd*, a much more ambitious one that had the worthy goal of eliminating the huge Russian bulge in the front south of the two Hungarian lakes. Aside from securing the oil fields, achieving that would have drastically shortened the front, thereby freeing up units for use elsewhere. It was a splendid idea, just as capturing Antwerp had been the previous December, and just as unrealistic.

Both *I. Kavallerie Korps* and *I. SS-Panzerkorps* had the initial objective of advancing to the Sio Canal between Mezokomarom and Simontornya, 15 to 25 km to the south. They would then cross the canal and move 60 km southeast until eventually closing on the western bank of the Danube, south of Budapest. *II. SS Panzerkorps* would be the offensive's left flank, with the mission of capturing Sárosd to secure that flank. *I Kavallerie Korps* was responsible for security of the far right flank, and for clearing the south bank of Lake Balaton.

III. Panzer Korps from Balck's *6. Armee* had the mission of defending the extreme left flank of the offensive, in the area of Stuhlweissenberg and Seregélys. Follow-on forces were virtually non-existent, as *Heeresgruppe Süd* had assigned its scant reserves to the assault formations; in particular, the shortage of infantry was acute. Available air cover was also minimal, although the Luftwaffe supported the offensive with anything airworthy. Exact numbers for tanks and assault guns available on the day of attack are hard to pin down. Reynolds' numbers for *I. SS-Panzerkorps* are listed above, but at the minimum some 278 tanks and assault guns were committed to the attack from all participating units of *6. SS-Panzerarmee*, with approximately 220 more in repair shops.[53] The chief reason for so many AFVs being unavailable was not only a breakdown in the manufacture, supply and transport of spare parts, but also to a collapse of internal communications. In some cases the parts existed and were in close proximity to the units that needed them, but either nobody knew it, or the supply officials would not release them without authorizations that never came.

---

[53] Guillemot, *Hungary*, pp 73

Considering the dire shortage of AFVs, fuel and ammunition, the Germans were playing a bad hand from the start. German logistics had never been able to supply an adequate stream of replacement parts, even before the factories had been bombed flat and the trains still ran on time, so in the event it's not hard to understand how the authorized strength of just the four SS Panzer Divisions in *6. SS-Panzerarmee*, which was approximately 640-800 AFVs, had been reduced to no more than 40 percent of that total combat-ready on March 6. In the event, as poor weather held up the armored vehicles and preventing them from leading the attack, the effect was that more AFVs were available in the second week of the offensive than the first. That was a testament to the repair crews who worked virtually around the clock to put as many vehicles as possible back into action.

Guillemot gives further evidence of just how committed Hitler was to *Unternehmen Frühlingserwachen* in a chart showing 39 percent of Germany's remaining armored forces concentrated in Hungary, vastly more than on any other front, with the bulk of those in *6. SS-Panzerarmee*.[54]

The details of the accepted plan called for *I. Kavallerie Korps* to attack on the right flank as *6. SS-Panzerarmee* drove south, securing that flank so the Panzer divisions could keep their strength at the point of attack, rather than being siphoned off for flank protection. Containing both *3. Kavallerie Division* and *4. Kavallerie*

---

[54] Guillemot, *Hungary*, pp 74

Division, I. Kavallerie Korps was a true mounted formation with few heavy weapons. It did not have the firepower necessary to accomplish its task of clearing the Russians from their entrencments south of Lake Balaton. Most of its armored component was made up of Hungarian 40M Nimrods, a tracked anti-aircraft vehicle mounting a 40mm gun. Essentially a copy of the Swedish Landsverk L-62 Anti II Self-propelled anti-aircraft gun, the Nimrod was a reasonably successful AFV in its intended role. By sheer necessity, however, it was pressed into the tank-dstroyer role, for which the main gun proved entirely unsuitable. When confronting strong Russian defenses during *Frühlingserwachen*, the Nimrods couldn't blast their way through and suffered heavy losses in the process.

Horses did give the corps mobility in the mud, but what they needed was artillery and tank support. To add further weight to its attack, *I. Kavallerie Korps* had part of the under-strength and demoralized Hungarian 25th Infantry Division attached, with the other half being assigned to *I. SS-Panzerkorps*. No regular Hungarian Army unit of this period was considered reliable, and none were anywhere close to full strength, with the sole exception of the elite and recently rebuilt Svent László Division. Motivated anti-communist Hungarians instead found a home in the Waffen-SS, in units such as *SS-Brigade Ney*.

A number of small units, and parts of units, had been attached to *I. SS-Panzerkorps*, including *Schwere-Panzer-Abteilung 509* fielding the powerful Tiger II. On their left was *II. SS-*

Panzerkorps. In addition to its two core divisions, *2. SS-Panzer Divisin Das Reich* and *9. SS-Panzer Division Hohenstaufen, II SS-Panzerkorps* also had under its command the under-strength *23. Panzer Division*, with 47 AFVs and 97 SPWs, and the average strength *44. Infanterie Division Hoch und Deutschmeister*.[55] All in all, the assault force was badly lacking in infantry and artillery, not to mention experienced leaders, fuel and ammunition.

The attack sector was in the zone of the Soviet Third Ukrainian Front[56], which was given extra ammunition to defend against the coming offensive, and had some 3,000 anti-tank weapons of all types, as well as almost 500 tanks. In effect, the Soviet defensive strategy was identical to what it had been at Kursk in July, 1943: allow the Germans to wear themselves out on the Soviet defenses, and counter-attack when the time was right.[57] In March of 1945, the form of that counterattack was planned as the Vienna Offensive, with the objective of capturing part or all of Austria.

One additional factor in the timing of the Russian counterattack was waiting until the ground dried out enough for large-scale tank movement. Since the Germans were attacking into an enormous bulge in the front, the further they advanced, the

[55] Guillemot, *Hungary*, pp 71
[56] Soviet 'Fronts' were the equivalent of German Army Groups.
[57] Guillemot, Hungary, pp 76-77

greater their danger of being cut off from the rear. The Russians wanted to make certain their armored forces could move fast enough to seal off any escape. In the event, they nearly were.

Unternehmen Frühlingserwachen began before dawn on March 6, with a short artillery bombardment, followed by *panzergrenadiers*[58] attacking the fixed Russian defenses. Like most such fortifications, they were built around the ubiquitous 76mm anti-tank gun as the center of a complex organization of machine gun nests and infantry trenches. A small collection of such guns was called a 'paknest', and a line of paknests was a 'pakfront,' with 'pak' being an abbreviation of the German word *panzerabwehrkanone*, or anti-tank gun.

With tanks sinking up to their turrets in mud, infantry struggling forward in waist deep sludge that sucked the boots off their feet, and soupy topsoil that muffled the effects of exploding artillery rounds, the surprise is not that the Germans made little progress, but that they made any progress at all. Relying on infantry was, at best, a short-lived solution to the problem of how to crack the Soviet defenses with the ground too soft for armor. Guillemot puts it succinctly when he says "this tank offensive would finally rapidly become an infantry battle, an element that was cruelly lacking with the 6th SS PzA."[59] Guillemot's point is succinct and well made. For

---

[58] Technically, the term *panzergrenadier* meant infantry that has been specially trained to operate with armored formations, using SPWs to keep pace with the panzers. In reality, by 1945 it meant infantry of any type.

the offensive to have achieved anything, it needed an immediate breakthrough and rapid exploitation. The exact opposite happened.

In effect, the battle became a slogging march in the mud, with *6. SS-Panzerarmee* blasting its way forward at the rate of a few kilometers per day. On the right flank, *I. Kavallerie Korps* did not have the firepower to advance and made little headway, but continued attacking regardless. On the left, as mentioned above, *II. SS-Panzerkorps* was delayed getting into attack position because of the weather, and did not even begin their advance until after 6 p.m. on March 6, more than 12 hours behind the rest of the army. As for *III. Panzerkorps*, under the command of Balck at *6. Armee*, it did not attack at all.[60] Nor did the attacks of *2. Panzerarmee* to the southwest, or the attacks in the south aimed at crossing the Drau (Drava) River, make significant progress; those attacks were so weak, in fact, that the Soviets did not have to use reserves to contain them, which meant those reserves could be used against *6. SS-Panzerarmee*. In places the Germans were driven back to their start lines on Day One.

Against all odds *I. SS-Panzerkorps* pushed through the Russian defenses, using AFVs when possible, and after 4 days of fighting began to close on Simontornya on the Sio Canal, their initial objective. On the right flank, *I. Kavallerie Korps* was only able to

---

[59] Guillemot, *Hungary*, pp 76-77
[60] Balck would later blame everything that went wrong in Hungary on Sepp Dietrich and the staff of *6. SS-Panzerarmee*.

push forward when *I. SS-Panzerkorps* success forced the Russians to retreat. Both German Corps had suffered heavy losses among the assault troops, however, and the attacks began to lose steam. On the left flank, *II. SS-Panzerkorps* had not only been stopped in its tracks at the town of Sárosd, its very first objective, and in spots it had actually lost ground to Soviet counter-attacks. Thus, as the offensive ground forward in the center, the left flank of *I. SS-Panzerkorps* was open for more than 20 km, which represented a clear and present danger. Nevertheless, advance units of *I. SS-Panzerkorps* crossed the Sio Canal and carved out a tenuous bridgehead on the southern side against fierce opposition. In Hitler's assessment this was a positive development, but in fact the opposite was true. The Germans could not hold any of the territory they took at such high cost, unless *II. SS-Panzerkorps* got underway. As things turned out, the failure of *II. SS-Panzerkorps* was the salvation of the army.

None of the commanders on the spot were blind to the imminent threat to the left flank of Balck's *6. Armee*, and all understood that the further they drove south, the more likely it was that the Russian Vienna Offensive could cut them off by securing the northeast tip of Lake Balaton. A change of plan was needed, but the problem was getting Hitler to agree. In a wily move that he has never been given credit for, Sepp Dietrich found the solution.

First, he requested to be allowed to use units from *I. SS-Panzerkorps* to attack Sárosd from behind, with the objective of breaking the Russian defenses and get those divisions moving. The

Soviet defenses were too much and only minor gains were made, but that wasn't the point, moving part of *I. SS-Panzerkorps* to the north was.

Having now failed at breaking Russian resistance around Sárosd, that left *6. SS-Panzerarmee* with just two viable options; first, it could renew the attack to the south along the Simontornya axis, an attack obviously going nowhere, or it could shift its forces northward to combine with *III. Panzerkorps* for an attack due east from the area of Stuhlweissenberg toward the Danube. Such a decision could only be made by Hitler, and he insisted on the offensive continuing as planned. Dietrich had planted the seed for an alternate line of attack, though, and that proved to be the salvation of his army.

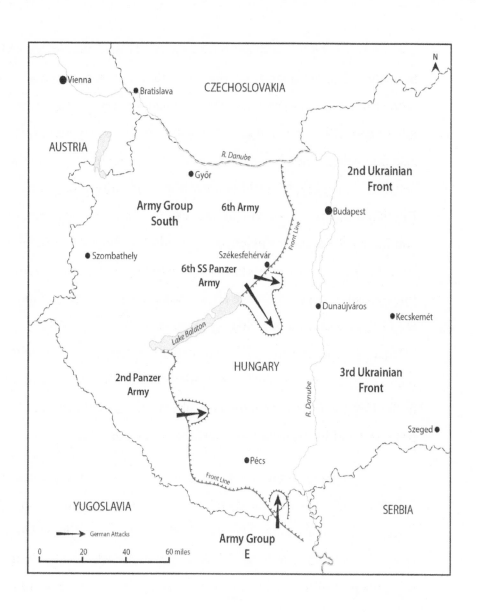

By this time both *Fremde Heeren Ost*[61], and the commanders on the spot, had no doubts the Soviet Vienna Offensive would be coming soon and in overwhelming strength. Hitler initially refused to believe this, but once again Sepp Dietrich's personal friendship with Hitler came into play. As Dietrich had already found out, any talk of cancelling the attack would be met with a stony *nein*. But he also knew that if he phrased things differently, he might yet get what he wanted, namely, to shift his army north to confront the coming Russian offensive. So in yet another cagey proposal, he suggested continuing the attack as planned, while also shifting more forces from *I. SS-Panzerkorps* north to help dislodge the Russians from the line Sárosd–Selegélyes. Once *II. SS-Panzerkorps* was on the move, the *Leibstandarte* units would again move south to rejoin the offensive at Simontornya. Alternatively, they could combine with all other mobile units and launch an armored tidal wave to reach the line of the Danube from the Stuhlweissenberg area, as he'd already proposed and had rejected. But Dietrich knew his man.

It was a brilliant variation on his earlier ruse, and it worked. On March 15, Hitler relented and agreed to the proposed shifting of forces for an attack to the Danube. *6. SS-Panzerarmee* immediately issued orders to begin the withdrawal, but of the whole army, not merely a part of it.[62] Given the narrow escape *Heeresgruppe Süd*

---

[61] Foreign Armies East was headed by master espionage organizer and intelligence analyst Reinhard Gehlen. After the war, Gehlen became a lynchpin in the covert American and West German bureaus spying on the Russians.

[62] Evidence is contradictory whether Hitler agreed to the withdrawal of the whole army, or merely part of it, but in the event it was

would have in the coming days, Dietrich's action saved it from destruction. Whether his critics were right and he was in over his head as an army commander, or it was jealousy for a man with no formal military training reaching such an exalted position, in that particular case Dietrich's intervention had far-reaching effects.

The withdrawal had only just begun when the long-expected Soviet Vienna Offensive began on the morning of March 16. Masses of Russian armor slammed into the demoralized and under-strength Hungarian Third Army in the Vertes Mountains just south of Gran. The weather had warmed by now and the fields were dry enough for mechanized units, which proved both good and bad for the Germans. And while mountainous terrain in the attack zone should have given the defenders the advantage, in fact the Russians made excellent progress against the outnumbered, outgunned Hungarians. There were no German or Hungarian reserves to counter-attack and within two days the Hungarian Third Army was routed and in danger of dissolution. Nor were the Soviet plans hard to discern: drive hard and fast for Balatonkenese, at the northeastern tip of Lake Balaton. Once they got there, every German to the east and south of that point would be trapped. As of March 16, that was all of *6. SS-Panzerarmee*. The race was on.

Just south of the collapsing Hungarian Third Army was the depleted *3. SS-Panzer Division Totenkopf*. At that point, *Totenkopf* had perhaps 10 operable AFVs. Seeing its left flank being turned, the

overtaken by events and became moot.

division began to bow its line to the west, trying to prevent being encircled, while simultaneously blocking a Russian thrust toward Lake Balaton. It was impossible, given *Totenkopfs* ruinously depleted state. So, since there were no reserves to plug the gap, or even to slow down the onrushing Red Army, the two under-strength *panzergrenadier* regiments from *Das Reich* were ordered north to try and buy enough time for the rest of *6. SS-Panzerarmee* to withdraw. Saving all of the army would have been impossible had Dietrich not tricked Hitler into granting him a precious day to start the process. Nevertheless, the *Das Reich* regiments had a mission that an entire army could not accomplish; stopping the Russian offensive. Next in line to *Totenkopf*, *5. SS-Panzer Division Wiking* and other German formations stood fast at Stuhlweissenberg, despite heavy attacks.

Thus began a desperate race to withdraw *6. SS-Panzerarmee* from the trap it had carved for itself, with the units flowing north and west while *6. Armee* units, notably *Totenkopf* and *Wiking*, tried to hold back the flood of Red Army units. This they did, standing their ground against impossible odds, along with *Das Reichs* two infantry regiments. It was an heroic achievement, but due to the odious nature of the respective governments involved, the remarkable determination displayed at Stuhlweissenberg has been forgotten by history. Regardless, despite their best efforts the Germans were pushed backward.

The crucial moment in the battle to save *6. SS-Panzerarmee* came early on the morning of March 20, at the railhead station in the small city of Veszprem. Located on the northern shore of Lake Balaton at the lake's northeastern tip, Veszprem was the key to the salvation of all German units to the south and east of the town. Had the Soviets seized Veszprem on the morning of March 20, most of *I. SS-Panzerkorps*, and all of *II. SS-Panzerkorps*, *IV. SS-Panzerkorps*, *I. Kavallerie Korps* and *6. Armee* would have been cut off and destroyed. *Heeresgruppe Süd* would have more or less ceased to exist as a cohesive fighting force, and would left no organized German resistance all the way to the Alps.

In an article from *Armor* magazine, Captain B. H. Freisen told the story of a nearly miraculous defensive fight saved most of Army Group South, and with it, Austria. Just outside Veszprem was the tiny village of Herend, the site of a railhead. That railway was designated to evacuate many of the German units in danger of being trapped by the Soviet offensive. In the pre-dawn darkness on March 20, the lead elements of *Das Reichs 2. SS-Panzer Regiment* pulled up to the railroad yards, and by mid-morning more than 40 of the regiments' tanks had assembled there and begun entraining.[63] The Regiment was in dire need of refit and repair after two weeks of fighting, and while Das Reich's two *panzergrenadier* regiments were trying to hold the broken front to the northeast, the precious tanks would be withdrawn by rail. As the first panzers rolled onto their platform-railcars, however, the lead elements of the Red Army,

---

[63] Friesen's article is one of our few references to panzer numbers for this period, although he does not list a source for the total.

racing for Veszprem through the gap where the Hungarian Third Army collapsed, rolled into sight and began to attack. With no infantry or artillery support, the panzers set up a makeshift defensive perimeter and fought back as best they could, while enduring heavy artillery fire and an air raid.

Over the next six hours they destroyed some 30-odd T-34s and hundreds of infantry, with some of the panzers engaging the enemy while still strapped down to the rail cars. The commander of one tank, *SS-Unterscharführer* Peter Rauch, told Captain Friesen what that was like. "As he approached the ramp, he saw the Panthers on the rail cars firing at the Russians, each shot rocking the cars violently". When the action ended, most of *Das Reich's* tanks escaped to a line further west, where they could repaired and used to keep the front from complete collapse.[64] When the fighting ended and the train pulled out for points west, it did so by stranding an entire company of panzers that hadn't yet arrived.

---

[64] Friesen, Captain B. H., (1988, XCVII (1). "Breakout from the Veszprem Railhead," *Armor, TheMagazine of Mobile Warfare,* pp 20-25.

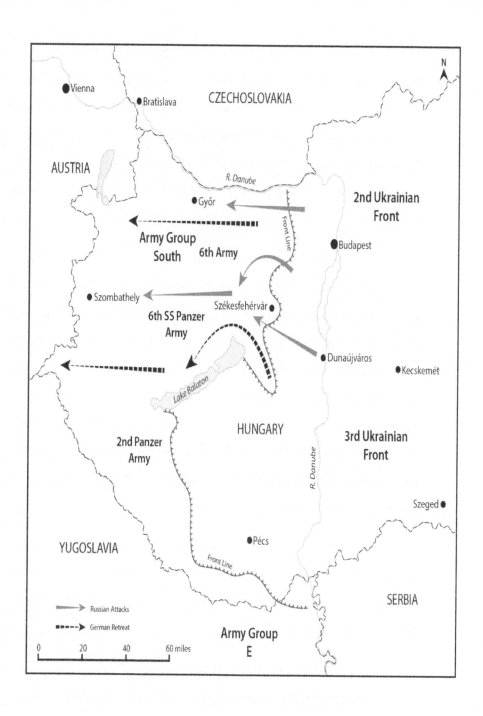

The Russians gave the two most powerful armies in *Heeresgruppe Süd* no respite, even after the near-miraculous stand of *2. SS-Panzer Regiment.* A corridor to the west only remained open because several formations resisted massive Red Army pressure and held it open at frightful cost, with *9. SS-Panzer Division Hohenstaufen* suffering particularly heavy casualties. At one point, the division commander himself picked up a weapon to fight.

Thereafter came a frantic retreat westwards by all surviving units of both *6. Armee* and *6. SS*-Panzerarmee, that never quite turned into a rout but also never found a place to form a defensible line; there were not enough German units to fill the gaps, and not enough fuel to allow the remaining units to maneuver. Armor and artillery losses were especially high during the last 10 days of March, because the Germans retreated too fast to set up fuel dumps even when fuel could be found. Vehicles that broke down and would usually have been repaired were instead destroyed to keep them away from the Russians.

To Hitler's ears these sounded like excuses, and with the failure of *Unternehmen Frühlingserwachen* he was not in a mood to forgive failure, so he looked for a scapegoat and found it in his old friend, Sepp Dietrich.

In early January, 1945, Hitler had made it clear that he was not disappointed with the performance of the Waffen SS divisions in the Ardennes Offensive. Maier quotes Hitler's adjutant, Otto

Günsche, as saying: "...I did not have the impression that the Führer blamed his disappointment over the failure of the Ardennes Offensive on the formations of the Waffen SS in particular."[65] In that same quote, however, Günsche does mention Hitler was aware of Frederick the Great's willingness to take awards and medals away from troops that he no longer believed deserved to wear them. By his testimony, we see the seed of Hitler's reaction to the failure of *Frühlingserwachen* as having already been planted. Undoubtedly so did Hitler's Army advisors.

The Waffen SS were, as the title of Tim Ripley's book used in this work suggests, *Hitler's Praetorians*. They were his Immortals, his Old Guard[66], one force he could always count on for unconditional support. Their founder, Hermannn Göring, was Deputy Führer after Rudolf Hess flew to Scotland in 1941, and his successor, Heinrich Himmler, created an entire mythology to support the idea of the SS being the Germanic ideal. The loyalty bond between the Führer and his Waffen-SS was proclaimed to be unbreakable.

Until the last two months of the war, that is.

---

[65] Maier, *Drama*, pp 112
[66] The Immortals were the elite force of the ancient Persian kings, maintained at a strength of 10,000 men, and served as the core of the mammoth armies Persia fielded against forces such as Greece. The Old Guard were Napoleon's most trusted veterans.

Casting around for scapegoats to explain the failure of Spring Awakening, followed by the desperate retreat in the face of the Soviet Vienna Offensive, and a performance in action that Hitler considered almost treasonous, he turned on his most loyal troops. Hitler ordered Dietrich's Waffen-SS men stripped of their prestigious cuff bands[67]. Based on faulty information, possibly fomented by jealous Army officers, a view that played into Hitler's increasingly paranoid outlook, the infamous Cuff Band Order essentially penalized the out-numbered and exhausted SS formations for not being able to accomplish the impossible.

The idea that false army reports caused the Cuff Band Order to be issued is backed up by the evidence. Minister of Propaganda and Enlightenment Joseph Goebbels tells us in his diary entry for March 27, 1945 "the army generals are rubbing their hands at the blow dealt to their rivals."[68] After the July 20, 1944 assassination attempt, Hitler had lost faith in the army and leaned ever more heavily on the Waffen SS. Yet the staff surrounding and advising him was entirely made up of army officers. The sole SS representative at Führer headquarters was Himmler's liaison officer, the vain and self-serving Hermann Fegelein, an ambitious man who would never endanger himself for the sake of his brother officers.[69]

[67] The irony of this order is that the cuff bands had been removed for the secret transfer to Hungary and had never been re-attached.
[68] Trevor-Roper, Hugh, editor, (1979), *Final Entries 1945, The Diaries of Joseph Goebbels*, (New York: Avon, 1979), pp 301

Additionally, the commander of *6. Armee* fighting alongside *6. SS-Panzerarmee*, Hermannn Balck, despised the Waffen SS. Even as he commanded *IV. SS-Panzerkorps*, Balck sent malicious reports about Dietrich's army to headquarters for weeks[70] before and during *Frühlingserwachen*. The failure of the offensive, and the subsequent retreat were enough to arouse Hitler's suspicions, but the worst claim made against Dietrich was that he intentionally withheld troops in Germany from the fighting in Hungary in anticipation of moving to the Berlin front, and against Hitler's direct order to use every available man in the attack. During a long talk with Hitler on March 27, Goebbels gives us the specifics of what angered Hitler, namely, that *6. SS-Panzerarmee* went into action with only 40,000 men instead of the 70,000 on its rolls, and that major formations were left in Germany.[71]

The perfidy of the Army in reporting this to the Führer shows how fractured the German High Command remained even when *in extremis*. The report has a kernel of truth, as such things usually do,

---

[69] Fegelein is sometimes referred to as Hitler's brother-in-law, since he married Gretl Braun, the sister of Hitler's mistress and future wife, Eva. Had Fegelein lived two more days he would have become Hitler's relative by marriage. However, on April 27, 1945, he was executed at Hitler's express order after being found with money and jewels, and his own mistress, ready to flee Berlin.
[70] In his memoirs, Balck continued to excoriate the SS and *6. SS-Panzerarmee* in particular. Maier was so angered that he wrote his book, *Drama Between Budapest and Vienna*, in response to what he considered unfair and inaccurate criticisms from Balck.
[71] Trevor-Roper, *Final Entries*, pp 310

but the number of men involved was 300, not 30,000. They were part of a replacement battalion of untrained men who arrived too late to ship out when the army transferred to Hungary. *6. SS-Panzerarmee* had at least 70,000 men on March 6, 1945.

It is instructive for those who want to understand the otherwise incomprehensible Cuff Band Order to study this dynamic. The generals involved knew first-hand that the war was irrevocably lost. The Third Reich was in its death throes and Hitler had just over one month to live, while in the west the Allies had been across the Rhine for three weeks and had *Heeresgruppe B* surrounded in the Ruhr Pocket; mere days later 430,000 Germans surrendered. In the east, the Russians had a bridgehead on the west bank of the Oder River, less than sixty miles from Berlin. Only the melting snows kept them at bay that long. And yet, in the insulated, Byzantine world of Hitler's inner circle, men still jockeyed for his favor, as if Germany was not being systematically overrun, while Army generals plotted vengeance on their hated SS rivals, even at the expense of the country.

As for the how the SS felt about their once-beloved Führer, times had changed. No longer did the troops view Hitler as a demigod. Dietrich's reaction to the Cuff Band Order was disgust and disobedience. Maier was the man on the spot when the order came in to *6. SS-Panzerarmee* headquarters, and personally handed the note to Dietrich. According to Maier, Dietrich told him not to pass on the order or speak of it, although others had also received a copy and its contents were soon known throughout the army. Maier goes on to relate the only person at Führer Headquarters to speak in defense of the Waffen SS was not Himmler, who was present, or Fegelein, whose job it was, but of all people Hermann Göring. The *Reichsmarshal* had fallen out of favor by this point, though, and he did not press his defense. The episode had little practical effect on the fighting. All those who learned of it, however, realized how little their sacrifices over the years had meant to Hitler and had the effect of destroying what little confidence remained in the German High Command.[72]

The last days of March and the first days of April found German formations retreating west, sometimes stopping to try and form a defensive line, but always at threat of being surrounded. Fuel shortages led many crews to blow up their vehicles when the Russians closed in and the fuel tanks were dry. Maintaining unit integrity in the face of overwhelming numbers was impossible, but somehow the Germans did not collapse, although the Red Army was pouring over the Austrian border by April 1. Moving rapidly, the Russians threatened to surround any German unit that stood to make a stand, pushing ahead of them a jumble of German and Hungarian military units, along with countless civilians, washed like flotsam on an outgoing tide.

---

[72] Maier, *Drama*, pp 302-305

Vienna had been designated by Hitler as a *festung*, a fortress, which was his standard procedure for threatened cities.[73] It made no practical difference beyond meaning that the city had to be defended to the last man, but the Führer's commands no longer carried the same weight as they once had. Over and over again both *Das Reich* and *Totenkopf* received a *Führerbefehl*[74] not to retreat from a given position and that it must be defended to the last man, and over and over again their commanders simply ignored Hitler's commands.

On April 2, with the city in a state of near panic, Sepp Dietrich was introduced on the radio as the defender of Vienna and promised to do everything in his power to stop the Red Army. Privately, he joked with Gauleiter[75] Baldur von Schirach the reason his army was called *6. SS-Panzerarmee* was because it only had six tanks left. He was exaggerating, but not by much: Weyr reports that on April 5 the whole army had 28 combat ready panzers.[76] This may or may not be an accurate number, and seems low, but perhaps this was the number for *II. SS*-Panzerkorps, which now had three panzer

---

[73] The "Fortress" designation meant the city had to be held to the last man and the last bullet, lest the commander on the spot be liable with his life and/or the lives of his family.

[74] Literally a Leader Order. These came directly from Hitler, and were inviolate on the penalty of death.

[75] Roughly speaking, a Gauleiter was governor of a region.

[76] Weyr, Thomas, *The Setting of the Pearl, Vienna under Hitler*, (New York: Oxford University Press, 2005), pp 275-276

divisions under its command, with *6. Panzer Division* being the third.

Regardless, even if the number of AFVS was doubled or even tripled, it contrasts sharply with June of 1944, when *I. SS-Panzerkorps* by itself listed some 376 AFVs, without including *II. SS-Panzerkorps* in the total. Indeed, things had become so chaotic and desperate that reinforcements intended for *12. SS-Panzer Division Hitlerjugend* were grabbed off their trains by men from *Das Reich* and put straight into the front lines. Some of those 2,800 men still wore the uniforms of their previous branch of service, either the *Kriegsmarine* or Luftwaffe, and were incorporated with no time to even get their names.

Throughout the first week of April, *6. SS-Panzerarmee* was shoved further and further apart. *II. SS-Panzerkorps* was pushed into Vienna and wound up being the primary defensive force in the city; by April 6 much of the corps was fighting in an arc, from the Danube to just south of Schönnbrunn Palace. Artillery batteries fired from with the palace courtyard. Meanwhile, *I. SS-Panzerkorps*, to the south and west of Vienna, made a stand in the foothills of the Alps.

Unknown to the defenders, however, a resistance group known as O-5 had contacted the Soviets and arranged a back-door entry into the city. Comprised of disillusioned Army personnel, units loyal to 0-5 were stationed in the Vienna Woods on the city's south and west as a defensive force. At a signal, they were supposed to move out of the way and allow the Red Army into Vienna from the west, thus outflanking the defenders. 0-5 was betrayed by carelessness before the plan could be put into operation, but it indicated how desperate many people were to save Vienna from destruction, and how unreliable many Wehrmacht forces had become.[77]

The Germans' unsolveable problem in defending Vienna was a paucity of forces, and the lack of firepower among those they did have. Third Ukranian Front broke through south of the city and attacked from west, southwest, south and east, with Second Ukrainian Front driving from the northeast, north of the Danube. The generals charged with defending the city never fooled themselves into believing it was possible, and resolved to give ground while exacting as high of a cost from the Russians as possible, but not to allow their men to be surrounded and destroyed for no purpose.

By April 12, *6. SS-Panzerarmee* was a shattered force scattered across East Central Austria. Despite the confusion, and the terrible losses and the Cuff Band Order and all of the other reasons the battered SS formations should have quit the battlefield, they

---

[77] Toland, John, *The Last 100 Days*, (New York: Bantam, 1967), pp 384-385

remained dangerous in the extreme. Nothing indicates this more than a possibly apocryphal incident in smoldering Vienna.

The city had been overrun south of the Danube except for a small perimeter still held around the Floridsdorf Bridge, the last bridge still spanning the Danube held by the Germans. Escape could only come via a narrow corridor leading north of the river, so the bridge was their only way out. There, some 700-1,000 men from *Das Reich* held back the Russians until the stacks of wounded sheltering in the lee of the bridge could be evacuated to the northern shore; Reynolds puts the number of wounded at 56.[78] Then, as historian David Porter put it "...*I. SS-Panzerkorps* delivered a sharp reminder of the tactical expertise of the dwindling number of veteran Panzer crews as the formation withdrew on the 12th - a single Panther of Das Reich, commanded by Leutnant Arno Giesen, knocked out 14 T-34s and JS-2s whilst holding one of the Danube bridges."[79]

The quote is interesting for two reasons: first it illustrates the ferocity of the fighting during that last day in Vienna. Whether it is the story of one Panther tank almost single-handedly saving the bridgehead and the scores of wounded SS men who were later evacuated almost becomes beside the point. Virtually unknown now, this vignette shows the difference one veteran SS man could make in the course of a titanic battle.

[78] Reynolds, *Sons*, pp 307
[79] Porter, David, *Order of Battle, The Red Army in WWII*, (London: Amber, 2009), pp 175

The second reason it's significant may be even more instructive, because the Panther tank in question was not commanded by Lieutenant Arno Giesen, as the commander was identified in the article written about this event. The commander was actually Arnold Friesen.

The confusion over identity was intentional and illustrates the difficulty latter day historians sometimes have in ferreting out the truth. With SS men in general being prosecuted after the war for various crimes, and with the SS as a whole being declared a criminal organization, many SS veterans changed their names, making verification of their wartime experiences difficult. This issue first cropped up with the quote John Toland used from 'Fritz Hagen' in the section about the weather in the lead up to *Unternehmen Frühlingserwachen*. Fritz Hagen is another alias, one for whom the true identity has never been established.

As Porter's quote above illustrates, even historians can be misled by the murk such deceptions cast over events. Nor was Friesen a minor figure; he concluded the war with 111 confirmed kills, making him one of the ten highest scoring German tank aces of the war.[80] The fog of deception comes from an interview Friesen gave to historian Peter R. Mansoor in the 1980's, detailing the events of April 12-13, 1945, in which he asked Mansoor to use the pseudonym Arno Giesen. Just like 'Fritz Hagen', whose name was not on the rolls of any Waffen SS Division, Friesen's deception

---

[80] If those kills in Vienna are added to his total, that is.

passed as truth, even though no Arno Giesen could be found on the rolls of *Das Reich*. Mansoor's article appeared in *Armor* magazine in 1986, when Arnold Friesen played his part in misdirecting an historical footnote.

While aspects of the action that makes this relevant have come into doubt in recent years, it should be noted that numerous military artists and writers have accepted it as fact during the years since it first came to light. It started on April 12, in the aforementioned pocket on the south bank of the Danube, a semi-circular perimeter based on the Floridsdorf Bridge. Friesen and his Panther tank were on the north side of the Danube, and were volunteered to cross the bridge into the perimeter holding out on the south side, bringing food and ammunition for the forces still fighting there. The bridge was under both direct and indirect Soviet fire, with a large hole in the center, so crossing in daylight was suicidal. Crossing under cover of darkness seemed marginally safer, since Soviet gunners rarely fired at night, but in utter darkness the hole in the bridge made it too dangerous. So, with consummate skill and covering fire from every available German artillery piece, and no small bit of luck, Friesen's tank made it safely across in daylight on April 12. The Panther tank he was re-supplying drove into a bomb crater, however, damaging it beyond repair.[81] Friesen was ordered to take its place supporting the bridgehead. There were only two tanks

---

[81] There is no dispute that the bridge had a large hole, adding to the veracity of the story.

left in the perimeter at that point, an older Mark IV guarding the western approach to the bridge, and Friesen's Panther guarding the eastern approach. Late on April 12 he took up a defensive position near the bridge and waited for daylight.

Russian tanks moved forward once day broke on April 13. Friesen directed the fire of his Panther and knocked out tank after tank, mostly T-34/85s, the upgraded version of the revolutionary design upon which the Panther itself was based. At least one, however, was reported to be a monstrous JS-II heavy tank.[82] Eventually, Friesen's tank suffered a turret hit that damaged its ability to rotate, so he and another crewman took some *panzerfausten*[83] and went in search of prey. After nightfall on the April 13 the two men attacked four T-34s in nearby Pater Abel Platz, just in front of the bridge, and destroyed two of them as the other two sped off back to their lines. All in all, Friesen and his Panther destroyed fourteen Russian tanks that day, blunting efforts to break through to the bridge and giving him a total of one hundred eleven

---

[82] Mansoor lists this as a JS-III in his article, which is impossible. Most likely it was a JS-II, the more numerous model on which the JS-III was based. There is little evidence the JS-III was used in World War II, however, just missing out on action by a few weeks. A few might have gotten into the fight at the end of the Battle of Berlin, but this has never been verified. Mansoor relied on Friesen's memory in his article.

[83] Plural of *panzerfaust*- the single-use, shaped charge anti-tank weapon upon which most modern rocket-propelled grenade launchers are based. This ubiquitous weapon was deadly in the hands of a man who knew how to use it, as Friesen's feats clearly showed.

kills by the end of the war. That night the SS men evacuated their wounded, pulled the last troops out of the bridgehead and blew up the bridge. At dawn on April 14, Vienna south of the Danube was entirely in Russian hands.

The fall of Vienna could have unhinged the German position north of the Danube, forcing the scattered pieces of *6. SS-Panzerarmee* fighting there, most notably *Das Reich*, to retreat west and yet it had the opposite effect. Heavy armored losses forced the Russian High Command, Stavka, to prioritize further moves, and they selected Czechoslovakia as the next most important objective. To seize that country before the Americans meant they first had to capture territory still held by the Germans around Zistersdorf, and that proved far more difficult, and costly, than anticipated.

The army headquarters and what was left of *I. SS-Panzerkorps* settled into a defensive posture in the mountainous Austrian interior south of the Danube, although a new concern made even that position seem untenable, namely, the Americans advancing from Italy and southern Germany into Austria. There is a myth that once Vienna fell nothing more happened in Austria, and that is patently untrue. Heavy fighting continued throughout April as the Russians only stopped attacking due to heavy losses, and the need to transfer units north for the fighting in Czechoslovakia. Not even four years of severe combat had made the Russians wary of taking unnecessary casualties, though, and attacks continued well into May. Even into the 21st Century, Russian families traveled to Austria to identify remains of possible relatives who were killed in an attack on May 1, 1945.

Finally, once it was clear they could not seize more of Austria, most large-scale attacks stopped. Small attacks in company strength continued in places, though, right up until the end. As for the Germans, by the first week in May, food, fuel and ammunition were in such critically short supply that the men in the units were effectively *hors de combat.* Some were literally starving.

Although the fighting in Hungary and Austria left *6. SS-Panzerarmee* virtually devoid of combat power, by May 8, the day of surrender, it had recovered somewhat under a flood of replacements. Food and war supplies remained inadequate, but a week of rest had a rejuvenating effect on the core Waffen-SS units of *6. SS-Panzerarmee. Das Reich* was missing, having been ordered north in a series of conflicting orders that left it strung out for more than one hundred miles. Only one *panzergrenadier* regiment stayed behind.

Aside from the continuing losses in men and vehicles to Russian gunfire and air attack, vehicles continued running out of fuel and being abandoned, usually (but not always) destroyed by their own crews. Like so many other issues in the campaign, the final strength of the SS divisions when the war ended remains open to debate. Some reported totals have been repeated without comment, despite their accuracy being improbable.

1. SS-Panzer Division Leibstandarte provides a good example of the conflicting data. Thiele cites often used figures that at the time of its surrender on May 9, 1945, the division had: "...three operational tank hunter(s), 57 officers, 229 NCOs and 894 soldiers," for a total of 1,180 men of all ranks, less than ten percent of its authorized strength.[84] This total has been repeated in numerous histories, yet it cannot be correct.

Reynolds gives no firm figures, noting that when the division surrendered to the Americans many of them were simply waved on to the west, while the U.S. 71st Infantry Division recorded a total of 3,777 *LAH* men taken prisoner.[85] Using every reference and source currently available, the author estimates the true number between 7-9,000 men of all ranks. The same discrepancy exists in the figures for the other Waffen SS divisions.

The numbers are blurred by the replacements that fleshed out the divisions in the second half of April and the first week of May. If records were kept at all, they have since been lost.

Adolf Hitler killed himself on April 30 and the surrender was signed on May 7, to take effect the next day. Yet the German replacement system still functioned to a surprising degree. On May 2 members of *SS-Schwere-Panzer Abteilung 509*, attached to *6. SS-Panzerarmee*, were directed to take possession of six *Jagdtigers*, the

---

[84] Thiele, *Beyond Monsters*, pp 264
[85] Reynolds, *Men*, pp 282

mammoth tank destroyer that mounted a 128mm cannon, the largest gun Germany used on an AFV during the war. No Allied tank, Russian, British or American, could withstand a hit from such a gun.

Building a *Jagdtiger* strained resources in late war Germany, yet there, at the end, were six brand new machines delivered too late to be of any use.[86] Nor is that an isolated incident. On May 7, *LAH* itself took possession of four factory fresh Mark IVs, which were promptly destroyed as the division prepared to surrender.[87] In late April, *23. Panzer Division* received a dozen brand new Mark IVs. Then, as if these examples were not surprising enough, Reynolds relates the surreal situation of *9. SS-Panzer Division Hohenstaufen*. The division was at least as badly damaged as its fellow divisions in *6. SS-Panzerarmee*, yet by the end of April *Hohenstaufen* was not only back up to its full authorized strength of 18,500 men, but might actually have been over-strength. The men ranged in age from seventeen to over sixty, they were by no means the superb physical specimens expected of Waffen SS soldiers, but somehow the replacement system had found the destination division in the Austrian interior and transported the men to there.[88]

---

[86] Less than 100 vehicles were built. Exact numbers are sketchy because of poor record keeping at the end of the war, but the final number is probably between 88 and 94.
[87] Reynolds, *Men*, pp 281
[88] Reynolds, *Sons*, pp. 302

An avalanche of evidence reinforces the belief that Josef Stalin intended for Austria the same fate as Poland. Free elections were promised, but the Russian dictator had no intention of allowing them to happen. Some critics have rejected this theory based on either a misunderstanding of the situation, or lack of familiarity with the evidence. Certainly those in the highest offices at the time didn't dismiss it so lightly, they feared that very thing.

On April 5, 1945, Winston Churchill wrote President Franklin Roosevelt about his concerns for the Red army overrunning Austria. He made no direct accusations of duplicity against Josef Stalin and the Soviet Union, but his implications were clear: "…we proposed…six weeks ago provisional zones of occupation in Austria, but since Yalta the Russians have sent no confirmation of these zones."[89] Clearly, the Russians delayed agreeing on how much of Austria to keep in their zone of control until they found out how much of Austria they could seize. There is now a convincing level of proof for this. Delving too deeply into the historical record is outside the scope of this essay, but is dealt with in detail in the author's book on the battle for Austria.

As one example of the Russian plans to set up a puppet Austrian regime to join the Warsaw Pact, on Stalin's orders the Russians in fact *did* create an Austrian government under their control, based in Vienna. At its head was the old socialist Karl

---

[89] Churchill, Winston S., *Triumph and Tragedy*, (Boston: Houghton Mifflin, 1953), pp. 512

Renner. It failed only because Churchill and Truman refused to recognize it, and the Russians did not conquer Austrian territory beyond the Line of Demarcation, as Churchill feared they might, because Adolf Hitler sent *6. SS Panzerarmee* to that theater of operations instead of to Berlin, or the Silesian Front.

As we have seen, his stated reasons for doing so were economic. Oil was the lifeblood of the Wehrmacht and the last sources of natural oil available to Germany were in Hungary and Austria. Committing his last offensive force to the mission of protecting those resources was universally opposed by his military advisors, but he was determined to carry through his plans for *Unternehmen Frühlingserwachen* and his was the only opinion that mattered.

In summation then, the truth of that cause is far less certain than it was in histories written closer to the war, as this essay has shown. On the surface, the notion that as an Austrian, Hitler placed protecting his homeland above protecting his capital city, and therefore himself, seems unlikely. And yet there is the previously quoted passage from Field Marshal Wilhelm Keitel that Hitler would rather lose Berlin than the oil area and Austria., leaving the lingering question that, if Keitel remembered Hitler's statement correctly, then why did the Führer include the words 'and Austria' in the debate about where best to deploy *6. SS Panzerarmee*? Austria did not, in and of itself, have anywhere near the strategic importance of Berlin, yet Hitler preferred saving his homeland to his capital? Why? The question is as intriguing as it is unanswerable.

If that seems thin evidence on which to base such a different theory from what has so commonly been accepted, there is more, as mentioned in the essay and elsewhere. Regardless of motives however, the effect of deploying *6. SS-Panzerarmee* to the southern theater of operations rendered moot the issue of what Stalin might have done had Austria been mostly or completely overrun by the Red Army and possibly, being incorporated into the Soviet sphere of influence as Churchill feared. Had such a thing come to pass, the entire landscape of the Cold War might have been changed, and with it, modern history.

Part of the fascination of history is wondering how things might have turned out differently, so the author hopes the reader will forgive a brief indulgence in speculation about how things might have differed had *6. SS-Panzerarmee* gone elsewhere.

The most likely use would have been as part of *Unternehmen Sonnenwende*, Operation Solstice, an armored attack launched on February 15, 1945, from the area of Stargard in Pomerania. *Generaloberst* Guderian's idea for the offensive was to drive into the right flank of Marshal Georgi Zhukov's First Belorussian Front, cut off its spearheads on the Oder River, and destroy them. From the beginning of its planning he anticipated *6. SS-Panzerarmee* being part of the attacking force, along with divisions evacuated from the Courland Pocket. Hitler approved the idea, as he did with most attacks, but denied the use of any units except those already in the area. Sepp Dietrich's *6. SS-Panzerarmee* would not be divered from Hungary, and the Courland Pocket would not be evacuated. Without the forces for a major offensive to save the capital, Guderian had to scale down *Sonnenwende* to an objective of relieving the city of Küstrin, on the east bank of the Oder River.

Guderian wanted 1,200 panzers for the offensive, but that number was far beyond Germany's capabilities at the time. Indeed, that number would have included every working panzer in the *Wehrmacht* Order of Battle, and then some. Noted above, roughly 4 out of every 10 combat ready AFVs was in Hungary during this period. Nor could food, fuel or ammunition have been scraped up to supply such a massive force. As it was, *11. SS-Panzerarmee* had only three days of fuel and ammunition for its scale-down attack force, and the offensive bogged down after an initial success, grinding to a halt after three days. Would *6. SS-Panzerarmee* have made a difference? Yes and no.

Transporting it north to the assembly area near Stettin should not have been more difficult than doing so to Hungary, especially since some parts of the army went through Berlin anyway. Nor would the jump-off date have been an issue, as it participated in *Unternehmen Südwind* beginning on February 17 in faraway Hungary. Assuming that additional fuel and ammunition could have been found, which it likely could not, the addition of nearly 300 more AFVs driven by veteran crews would surely have given the *Sonnewende* attack the weight it needed to fight through to Küstrin, and that is probaby what would have happened. But achieving the decisive victory that Guderian planned for seems like a repeat of the Ardennes Offensive, asking too much from too few.

Was the relief of Küstrin enough of a mission to warrant using Germany's biggest remaining armored asset? No. The Oder River would still have been the defensive line behind which the Germans would have had to make their stand, and Zhukov would still have spent two months clearing Pomerania of German forces. The decision would have had to have been made whether to use *6. Panzerarmee* in the defense of Königsberg or Stettin, where it certainly would have delayed the Russian conquest of those cities, but just as surely would have been ground up in the fighting, or to withdraw it behind the Oder to await the Battle of Berlin. Either way, whatever losses it suffered in Pomerania would have been impossible to make up.

Some generals wanted it brought north to defend Berlin, and not used before the decisive battle, but this seems the least likely scenario. It was against everything Hitler believed in not to use every resource in the attack, as had been previously discussed. Had this occurred anyway, and the army allowed two months to repair equipment, train new replacements and add wounded veterans back from convalescence, its combat value would have once again been formidable. Whether *I. SS-Panzerkorps* and *II. SS-Panzerkorps* would have fought together, or one been used north of the city and the other to its south, the Russians would have paid a much higher price for Berlin's capture than the terrible cost they historically did pay. What would not have changed was the inevitable result of Hitler dead, and Nazi Germany defeated.

The other option was to leave *6. SS-Panzerarmee* where it was, west of the Rhine River, to oppose the Western Allies. If Hitler had allowed it to be used as a counter-attacking force, then it could have made the advance to the Rhine bloodier than it was, but it should be remembered that American and British air power made all daylight movements difficult. The very thing that made a tank army valuable, its mobility, acted as a disadvantage during daylight. American and British ground attack aircraft roamed deep into German airspace looking for targets, and would have taken a heavy and relentless toll to drain away the army's strength. Hitler forbade an early withdrawal across the Rhine and lost most of his forces as a consequence. *6. SS-Panzerarmee* would have increased the cost of clearing the west bank of the Rhine, but again could not have been a decisive factor. The Western Allies were too strong.

What effect would an alternate deployment of *6. SS-anzerarmee* had on the fate of Austria? It would have changed everything.

Without *6. SS-Panzerarmee* there could not have been an *Unternehmen Frühlingserwachen*. That would have been a net positive for the Germans, in that they suffered heavy losses for no meaningful gain, but Hermann Balck's *6. Armee* would have been no better able to withstand the Russian Vienna Offensive than it was. Without *Das Reichs* two regiments to hold back the flood, and *Hohenstaufen* to hold open an escape corridor, Balck might easily have lost half or more of his best troops at the outset. Even with *6. SS-Panzerarmee* the German front in Austria had major gaps that were exploited by the Red Army; without Dietrich's command, it seems impossible that the Germans could have done more than retreat into Western Austria and cede the rest with little or no resistance. The units available were simply too weak and too few to do more.

Marshal of the Soviet Union Fyodor Tolbukhin, commander of Third Ukrainian Front, was long known to have a dream of driving down the Danube Valley all the way to Munich. That was the natural invasion route of armies moving west or east in South-Central Europe. Once his armies fought past Sankt Pölten in Austria, it became obvious that still remained his ultimate objective, but the German defense, led by *6. SS-Panzerarmee*, stopped him. Had his Front not had to batter their way into the foothills of the Alps in Eastern Austria, or spend two weeks capturing Vienna, there would have been very little to stop him from accomplishing that dream, likely forcing Eisenhower to divert Patton into Bavaria into of Czechoslovakia.

The ultimate question then becomes whether or not Stalin would have given back Austrian territory in the American and British zones of occupation, or manufactured an excuse to keep them, such as a 'free election' by the people to remain under Soviet control. Against Churchill's pleadings to prevent this very thing, first Roosevelt and then Truman ordered American forces to stop at the demarcation line. They had no territory of their own to trade Stalin for the parts of Austria they rightfully should have occupied, and, as shown above, the Russians installed a pro-Soviet government even without accomplishing their greater objective. There seems no reason to believe Stalin would have shown greater faith had his bargaining position been stronger.

To those who disbelieve such a thing could happen, it requires only a look at the situation to understand how Stalin could have seen an opportunity. From virtually the moment the war ended the United States demobilized and transferred forces out of Europe. Among the combat formations, men with the most points were shipped home first. Points were accumulated in a new of ways, but by and large they were the most experienced troops. Veteran and reliable combat formations quickly lost combat power as untested replacements refilled their ranks.

The Army Air Forces moved even faster to the Pacific, to prepare for the invasion of Japan. Heavy bombers of the 8th and 15th Army Air Forces found new bases in northern Okinawa. Many fighter and ground attack groups moved too, while the best pilots were allowed to muster out if they so chose. There was no appetite for starting a new war against America's erstwhile ally, Russia, either in the United States or in Britain.[90] As for President Truman, who was far less favorably disposed to the Soviet Union than was Roosevelt, he only took power on April 12, 1945 and had little political capital to spend on a new war. Stalin knew all of this through his extensive spy network in America, just like he knew in advance that the United States had an atomic bomb program, so that when Truman announced a successful detonation while at Potsdam in July, 1945, Stalin wasn't surprised. But he was impressed, and given the overall situation he chose to shift his forces to the Far East, where Manchuria and Korea were ripe for the taking, along with the southern half of Sakhalin Island and maybe even Japan's northernmost island, Hokkaido.

Did Hitler intend to protect his homeland, rather than his shattered capital? It seems unlikely to the point of being preposterous, and yet Hitler *was* sentimental, sometimes to the point of being mawkish. If there was any truth to the idea of valuing his

---

[90] Churchill was voted out of power in July, after all, as the British were far more concerned with social programs than further fighting, particularly since the victorious Labour Party and its supporters looked upon Stalin as a friend.

homeland more than his capital, then it is possible that Hitler himself didn't consciously realize it. Regardless of why however, whether it was intentional or merely a consequence of transferring *6. SS-Panzerarmee* to Hungary, the effect was the same; the SS divisions bought enough time for the Americans to arrive at the demarcation line in Austria before the Russians did.

The End

Selected Bibliography

Bünau, General der Infanterie Rudolf von, *Kriegsgeschichtlicher Bericht von General der Infanterie Rudolf von Bünau über das Korps von Bünau von April bis Mai 1945, Juli 1946*, https://wwii.germandocsinrussia.org/de/nodes/3720-akte-789-#page/1/mode/grid/zoom/1, retrieved March 23, 2021.

Churchill, Sir Winston S., *Triumph and Tragedy*, (Boston: Houghton Mifflin, 1953).

Guillemot, Phillippe, translated from the French by Lawrence Brown, *Hungary 1944-45, The Panzers'Last Stand*, (Paris: Histoire & Collections, 2010).

Guderian, Heinz, *Panzer Leader: The Classic Account of German Tanks in World War II – by the Commander of Hitler's Panzer Corps in Russia*, (New York: Ballantine, 1968).

Maier, Georg, translated from the German by Robert E. Dohrenwend, *Drama Between Budapest and Vienna, The Final*

Battles of the 6. Panzer-Armee in theEast – 1945 (Winnipeg: J.J. Fedorowicz, 2004).

Porter, David, *Order of Battle, The Red Army in WWII.* (London: Amber, 2009).

Rauchenstiener, Manfred, *Schriften des heeresgeschichtlichen museums in Wien band 5 krieg in Ossterreich 1945*, (Wien: Osterreichischer Bundesverlag Fur Unterricht, Wissenschaft und Kunst, 1970).

Reynolds, Brigadier General Michael, *Sons of the Reich, II SS Panzer Corps*, (Havertown: Casemate, 2002).

> *Steel Unferno: I SS Panzer Corps in Normandy*, (New York: Sarpedon, 1997).

> *Men of Steel: I SS Panzer Corps, The Ardennes and Eastern Front 1944-45*, (New York: Sarpedon, 1999).

Ripley, Tim, *The Waffen-SS at War, Hitler's Praetorians 1925-1945*, (St. Paul: Zenith Press, 2004).

Thiele, K. H., *Beyond "Monsters and Clowns", The Combat SS: Demythologizing Five Decades of German Elite Formations*, (Lanham: University Press of America, 1997).

Toland, John, *The Last 100 Days*, (New York: Bantam, 1967).

Tooze, Adam, *The Wages of Destruction,The Making and Breaking of the Nazi Economy*, (New York: Viking, 2009).

Trevor-Roper, Hugh, editor, *Final Entries 1945, The Diaries of Joseph Goebbels*, (New York: Avon, 1979).

Warlimont, General Walther, translated From the German by B. H. Barry, *Inside Hitler's Headquarters 1939-1945* (Novato: Presidio Press, 1990).

Weyr, Thomas, *The Setting of the Pearl, Vienna under Hitler*, (New York: Oxford University Press, 2005).

Periodicals

Mansoor, First Lieutenant P. R., (1986, XCV(1). "The Defense of the Vienna Bridgehead," *Armor, The Magazine of Mobile Warfare*, 26-32.

Friesen, Captain B. H., (1988, XCVII (1). "Breakout from the Veszprem Railhead," *Armor, TheMagazine of Mobile Warfare*, 20-25.

Goda, N. J.W. (2000), "Hitler's Bribery of His Senior Officers During World War II," *The Journal of Modern History, 72(2)*, 413-452, retrieved March 8, 2011, from jstor database.

Koehl, R., (1962), "The Character of the Nazi SS," *The Journal of Modern History, 34(3)*, 275-283, retrieved March 8, 2011, from jstor database.

Reynolds, Major General Michael, (2009), *"Unternehmen Frühlingserwachen*: Adolf Hitler's Last WW II Offensive," *World War II Magazine, May 2009.*

Weinberg, G. L. (1993), "German Plans for Victory, 1944-45," *Central European History, 26(2),* 215-228, retrieved March 8, 2011, from jstor database.

(1968), "Sepp Dietrich, Heinrich Himmler, and the Leibstandarte SS Adolf Hitler, 1933-1938," *Central European History, 1(3),* 264-284.

(1945). *War Department Technical Manual TM-E30-451 Handbook on German Military Forces, 15 March, 1945.* I-57, Washington: War Department, retrieved February 22, 2011, from http://www.ibiblio.org/hyperwar/Germany/HB/HB-1.html,

Wood, James A., (2005), "Captive Historians, Captive Audience: The German Military History Program, 1945-1961,"*The Journal of Military History, 69(1),* 123-147, retrieved March 8, 2011, from the jstor database.

Follow information on new releases, subscribe to the author's newsletter at https://www.thelastbrigade.com or follow him on Bookbub.com.

Made in the USA
Las Vegas, NV
30 March 2024

88010695R00059